What others

The Barr

Given the risky and pioneering nature of church planting, it is essential to develop healthy relationships amongst members of the founding team. Here J. D. Payne gives us a biblical model of engendering healthy team dynamics by looking to the life and ministry of Barnabas. This is a book for those of us who want to keep a joyful camaraderie whilst advancing the kingdom.

Alan Hirsch
Author of *The Forgotten Ways* and *The Shaping of Things to Come*
Founding director of Shapevine.com

The Barnabas Factors: Eight Essential Practices of Church Planting Team Members is a unique and much needed book for anyone interested in church planting. I strongly believe it is a must-read for newly appointed missionaries and just as essential for veteran missionaries. This book powerfully sets forth the need for godly personal characteristics that are vital for successful church planting teams. The diagnostic tool at the conclusion of the book will be a great help in evaluating potential team members.

Charles Brock
President, Church Growth International
Author of *Indigenous Church Planting: A Practical Journey*

I highly recommend this book. From end to end it is practical: it's the relationship stuff, the personal qualities of team members, and the realistic nuts and bolts of ministry that are so ultimately determinative to fruitfulness in the church planting and team contexts. Payne brings great clarity as to what is a missionary "call." And for no extra charge there is a powerful tool at the end pulling all the principles together to help you decide who to take onto your team and who not to. A must-read for all church planters.

Daniel Sinclair
Author of *A Vision of the Possible: Pioneer Church Planting in Teams*

You reproduce what you are! In The *Barnabas Factors: Eight Essential Practices of Church Planting Team Members*, J. D. skillfully uses Barnabas to expose eight critical factors that enable a person to be an effective team player. Often, in the West we focus on glittery leaders; J. D. focuses on Barnabas, the glue of Paul's first team. He does an excellent job of making these attributes practical and applicable in the team church planting context . . . The book certainly should be read by those headed for the field and those teams already functioning in a field context.

Dick Scoggins
Head of Leadership Development, Frontiers
Author of *Building Effective Church Planting Teams*

Dr. J. D. Payne stresses the crucial need for possessing the personal and character qualities that were evident in the life and ministry of Barnabas. I wholeheartedly recommend this book to those who are dead serious about planting churches that are built on a solid biblical foundation and impacting their communities in the same manner in which the churches started by Barnabas and his team members impacted theirs.

Daniel R. Sanchez
Director, Scarborough Institute for Church Planting and Growth,
Roy Fish School of Evangelism and Missions,
Southwestern Baptist Theological Seminary

Having served as a church-planting missionary and trainer church planters for over twenty years, I believe the greatest obstacles to effective church planting teams were, and today remain, unresolved team conflict and personal character issues of team members. Now there is a tool to help church planters be more proactive in effectively selecting suitable team members. If there is a priority need today in church planting, it is a need for the church planting team members first to be people of exemplary Christ-like character . . . Payne's book addresses this issue in a clear and concise manner. This tool is a necessity for every church planter's, mission agency's, and church's toolkit as they seek to develop and deploy effective church planting teams for the glory of God.

R. Bruce Carlton
Associate Professor of Missions,
Boyce College
Author of *Acts 29: Practical Training in Facilitating Church-Planting Movements Among the Neglected Harvest Fields*

J. D. Payne offers sound biblical advice for building a strong church planting team. Often, in an attempt to build the perfect "Dream Team" many church planters rush the process and end up shipwrecking the potential of a new church. Nothing can be more devastating to the birth of a new church than a spiritually dysfunctional team. Whether you are planting a new church or leading a church planting organization, *The Barnabas Factors: Eight Essential Practices of Church Planting Team Members* is a must-read!

Stephen Gray
National Missions Director for the General Association of General Baptists
Author of *Planting Fast Growing Churches*

t seems J. D. Payne has been reading the New Testament again. The author's new book, *The Barnabas Factors*, is a helpful addition to church planting literature. Most mission agencies encourage or require their personnel to work in teams, yet few train their personnel to function effectively in a team format. This book would make an excellent resource for agencies to use with their church planters. The team members could study this book together and thus avoid the many problems that beset church planting teams. Mission leaders should thank J. D. Payne for providing positive solutions to a vexing problem.

Mark Terry
Visiting Professor of Missions,
Malaysia Baptist Theological Seminary;
Adjunct Professor of Missions,
The Southern Baptist Theological Seminary

Dr. J. D. Payne's book *The Barnabas Factors: Eight Essential Practices of Church Planting Team Members* should be on the "must-read" list for every church planter. Whether you are in seminary, already planting, or have the dream in your heart, you need to read this book. This is the way for a planter to find his dream team. I am not talking about a team with incredible talent. I am talking about a team that has what it takes to push back the forces of darkness! Build your team on the principles in J. D.'s book. If you do, I believe you will see great advancement of the Kingdom of God.

Gary Smith
National Missionary to Canada,
North American Mission Board

The Barnabas Factors: Eight Essential Practices of Church Planting Team Members

By

J. D. Payne

MISSIONAL PRESS

Published by Missional Press
149 Golden Plover Drive
Smyrna, DE 19977
www.missional-press.com

Printed in the United States of America

All Scripture quotations, unless otherwise noted, are taken from The
New American Standard Bible®, Copyright © 1960, 1962, 1963, 1968,
1971, 1972, 1973, 1975, 1977, 1995 by The Lockman Foundation.
Used by permission. www.Lockman.org

ISBN-10: 0-9798053-4-1
ISBN-13: 978-0-9798053-4-9

Cover design by Creative Juice

Table of Contents

To the Great Encourager

and

to Sarah

Acknowledgements

When I wrote my first book, *Missional House Churches,* I was surprised to discover how much of publishing a book is actually a team effort. Now that I have completed this sophomore project, I can still attest to this fact: no author can publish a good book without the assistance of others. I guess it is only appropriate that this point was brought to my attention once again while I was working to publish this book on teams.

For me to begin by thanking the Lord for His provision and leadership in the writing of this book is not a statement that I write flippantly, as if I am receiving a Grammy Award and such is the thing to do before a crowd. Rather, I recognize that He is my Lord and guides me in all that I do, including my writings. He was the One who put together the first church planting team with Barnabas and Paul. And I am thankful that, two thousand years later, I could have the honor of writing about that apostolic pattern. Much thanksgiving is due to Him for this work.

The Lord has used numerous conversations over the years to spark my curiosity for writing a book about church planting teams. I greatly appreciate my students, friends, and colleagues at The Southern Baptist Theological Seminary and the North American Mission Board for providing such encounters over time. Also, I regularly work with numerous church planting leaders and church planters, particularly across the Southern Baptist Convention. Working with them has also been a factor in the development of this work. To all of these folk I say thank you.

I also greatly appreciate men like Dick Scoggins, Daniel Sinclair, and Greg Livingstone. Prior to the writing of this book, these three wrote the few influential works championing the need for a team approach to church planting. Thank you, gentlemen, for your Kingdom service.

Much appreciation goes to Kari Plevan, my secretary in the Church Planting Center at The Southern Baptist Theological Seminary. She transcribed a great portion of this book from my dictation and assisted with a few other components as well. Thank you very much, Kari. It is a pleasure working with you to see the gospel carried across North America and beyond.

Joel Rainey and David Jackson have been two great encouragers to me and have also been advocates for *The Barnabas Factors* as I was seeking to publish it. Thank you, gentlemen, for your words of exhortation and assistance in this journey. These men truly have a heart for church planting teams.

David Phillips and Erin Amundsen with Missional Press are to be commended. David and Erin also have been great encouragers to me. Thank you, David (and the review board with Missional Press), for your willingness to publish this work. David and Erin, I greatly appreciate your professionalism and knowledge of the publishing industry. Keep up the great work.

Valery Gresham has been my editor for this project. She has done an incredible job. Though at the end of the day, I take full responsibility for the contents of this work, Val's work has been greatly appreciated. Val, it has been a blessing working with you. Your attitude and service for the Kingdom are incredible. Thank you for your contribution to this work.

Thank you, Kate with Creative Juices. Your expertise has been a great asset to this work. Thank you, Dave Wetzler with Church Smart Resources. You were an encouragement to me and provided me with some excellent guidance along the way. Thank you, Rad Zdero, for your words of encouragement and support early in the journey of this work.

Last, but most definitely not least, I must thank Sarah, Hannah, Rachel, and Joel. These four make the Payne household complete. I am very thankful for you guys and love you greatly. Your encouragement, prayers, and support in this writing endeavor are priceless. I believe we make a great team together.

Foreword

In this book, *The Barnabas Factors: Eight Essential Practices of Church Planting Team Members*, J. D. Payne addresses the desired characteristics of team members in the context of church planting teams. He does this by examining the life of Barnabas in Christianity's first church planting efforts.

This book is different from anything I've seen in church planting books. While it is generally expected that a book will start with a concept and then move to the use of scriptures to back up that concept, J. D. takes a completely different approach. This is a very straightforward, non-glitzy look at what the Bible has to say about team ministry in church planting. The principles laid out and explained in this book are taken directly from the scriptures through an in-depth look at the life and ministry of Barnabas.

It's not really a revolutionary idea to draw one's understandings from the biblical text, but it is a foundational principle that we often miss in our quest for effective leadership and exponential growth. The primary reference point for J. D.'s book is a candid look at biblical references to Barnabas. To put it simply, the primary case study for this book is the life and ministry of Barnabas.

Case studies can be powerful. They give us insight into the motivations, principles, and goals of the one being studied, while allowing us a window for viewing our own circumstances through the filter of someone else's experience. By looking at the biblical principles in Barnabas' life and ministry, this book has a high scriptural component that provides an even clearer window into your own church planting experience. After all, nothing is able to speak to the soul like God's Word. Similarly, when we think of church planting in the Bible, we might easily be drawn to the more-famous Paul. Yet as you read the words of this book, you will find that Barnabas's experiences aren't too far removed from your own planting journey. He wasn't the star. He was more like most of us—an ordinary guy who surrendered to a great call to simply do his best to assist in the greatest mission enterprise ever.

Barnabas probably lacked some of the oratory skills or apologetic artistry of more famous guys like Peter or Paul, but Barnabas's faithfulness provides a glimpse into how we can be better church planters in a calling that is often trying and always in need of greater staying power, faith, and steady determination.

Through an examination of Barnabas's life and ministry, J. D. has identified eight characteristics of successful church planting team members. He applies these characteristics not only to the individual church planter, but also to the church planting team. He then examines each of these characteristics in detail and helps the church planter apply them to the everyday needs of the church planter and his team.

As you read this book, you will come to a greater understanding of these biblical qualities. This understanding will aid you in either building an effective team from scratch or in reforming your present staff to function and live as a team.

Although *The Barnabas Factors* is not a how-to book or a strategy manual for the team approach in church planting, J. D. has provided a very nice and concise application section at the end of each chapter entitled, "Points to Ponder for Team Development."

I personally believe this application section is one of the best features of this book. These questions are designed for the church planting team members to use in sharpening their own application of the principles taught in this book. It would greatly benefit you and your team to systematically study and discuss these "Points to Ponder for Team Development" during your weekly training/staff time. Another good option might be to use these reflection questions in a retreat or weekend training event for your team.

As you read this book and continue along your church planting journey, let me encourage you to always center all that you are and all that you do on the gospel. As you prayerfully strategize on how to employ the knowledge gained in this book in your own team setting, keep the message of the gospel front and center. J. D.'s methodology for extracting his material straight from the scriptures is a good reminder for us to always, always, always keep the proclamation of the gospel as our chief purpose.

May God greatly bless you and work through you as you assemble and grow a team for a great harvest.

Ed Stetzer, Ph.D.
www.newchurches.com

Introduction

"Two are better than one because they have a good return for their labor. For if either of them falls, the one will lift up his companion. But woe to the one who falls when there is not another to lift him up. Furthermore, if two lie down together they keep warm, but how can one be warm alone? And if one can overpower him who is alone, two can resist him. A cord of three strands is not quickly torn apart" (Ecclesiastes 4:9–12).

When the opera superstar Luciano Pavarotti died in late 2007, droves of mourners gathered near his home in northern Italy. Pavarotti made opera accessible and enjoyable for the masses, and people loved him for that.

Even those who are not opera fans have probably heard of Pavarotti's name in conjunction with José Carreras and Plácido Domingo; these men comprised the famous "Three Tenors." The following story was told about the trio and their unity on stage:

> The November 1994 issue of *Atlantic Monthly* reported that prior to their performance in Los Angeles, a journalist tried to press the issue of competitiveness between the three men. But they quickly disarmed him.
> "You have to put all of your concentration into opening your heart to the music," Domingo said. "You can't be rivals when you're together making music."[1]

This simple yet profound statement revealed the philosophy of this musical team. Cooperation, rather than

---

[1] John C. Maxwell and Tim Elmore, *The Power of Partnership in the Church* (Nashville, TN: J. Countryman, 1999), 15.

competition, was critical to the overall health and vitality of the work of these men.

The Bible is filled with examples of teams co-operating for God's glory. Moses and Aaron, Elijah and Elisha, David and Jonathan, and Jesus and His twelve disciples are just a few examples. Luke records that teams also formed the majority of the missionary workforce of the early churches. Paul worked with Barnabas, John Mark, Silas, and Timothy throughout the book of Acts. David W. Shenk and Ervin R. Stutzman observe that team co-operation was typical in the Apostolic Church era. They comment: "Nevertheless, it is also true that when the believers reached out through church planting, the Acts record suggests that the ministry was always carried forward by a team. They apparently never commissioned a missionary to go alone into a new region to plant churches."[2]

In God's economy, the team was and is vital to the propagation of the gospel and the multiplication of disciples, leaders, and churches.[3] Not only was the team paradigm an expectation in the scriptures, but it was also a means to

---

[2] David W. Shenk and Ervin R. Stutzman, *Creating Communities of the Kingdom: New Testament Models of Church Planting* (Scottdale, PA and Waterloo, Ontario: Herald Press, 1988), 43–44.

[3] Throughout this work, when I refer to the local church, I will use the word with a lowercase "c". However, I will use an uppercase "C" when referencing the universal Church, a denomination, or the Church in a country or on a continent (e.g., North American Church).

accomplish more than the individual sum of its parts (Eccl. 4:9–12).

Not Just Another Book on Team Ministry

Though other authors have written on the concept of team ministry, few resources exist related to team ministry and church planting. At present, three of the few such resources are Daniel Sinclair's *A Vision of the Possible: Pioneer Church Planting in Teams* (Waynesboro, GA: Authentic Media, 2005); Greg Livingstone's *Planting Churches in Muslim Cities: A Team Approach* (Grand Rapids, MI: Baker Academic, 1993); and Dick Scoggins's unpublished manuscript, *Building Effective Church Planting Teams* (available at www.dickscoggins.com). *The Barnabas Factors* is an attempt to not only fill in the gap in church planting team literature but also to approach the concept of team from a different angle—how the personal characteristics and practices of team members contribute to effective church planting.

This book does not attempt to persuade the reader to consider using a team approach to planting churches. For such material, I must defer to Sinclair, Livingstone, and Scoggins. This book is built on the assumption that the reader is already convinced of the necessity and value of the team paradigm.

This work does not address the steps involved in forming a church planting team. Again, I defer to Scoggins on this topic. He has produced an excellent "Covenant of Team Understandings" which I have included in Appendix 1. Also, there are numerous works that explicitly address team ministry in established churches.[4] Many of these resources contain principles that are translatable to missionary contexts and can be applied to church planting.

This is not a book about church planting methodology and strategy. Aside from focusing on the team paradigm, I do not address how to plant churches. I also do not address what knowledge and practical church planting skills are necessary for effective teams. Most current church planting texts deal with these issues.[5]

The reader should not be naïve and think that by following the teachings of this book he will avoid any future problems with the church planting team.[6] Though this work has much to offer teams, I am not under the illusion that this work is a panacea for all troubles.

---

[4] For example, Kenneth O. Gangel, *Team Leadership in Christian Ministry,* revised (Chicago, IL: Moody Press, 1997); George Barna, *The Power of Team Leadership: Finding Strength in Shared Responsibilities* (Colorado Springs, CO: WaterBrook Press, 2001); and Wayne Cordeiro, *Doing Church as a Team: The Miracle of Teamwork and How It Transforms Churches* (Ventura, CA: Regal, 2001).
[5] For example see my forthcoming work tentatively titled *Discovering Church Planting: An Introduction to the What's, Why's, and How's of Biblical Church Planting* (Colorado Springs, CO: Paternoster, 2009).
[6] While I believe that church planting teams may consist of men and women, I have chosen to use the masculine pronoun to avoid the awkwardness of constantly including both masculine and feminine pronouns.

The Unique Focus of This Book

The unique focus of this book is the use of Barnabas as a model for assessing the personal characteristics and practices of church planters. This work addresses a critical element in missions that is often overlooked: the necessary personal character qualities and practices of effective church planters. In this book, I use Barnabas as an example for contemporary missionaries.[7]

Though this work primarily focuses on the biblical texts revolving around the life of Barnabas, each chapter assists missionaries in applying the concepts to their lives and their teams. Team reflection questions and the insights and experiences from contemporary church planters are included in each chapter. In the conclusion of this book, I attempt to bring together all of the chapters and provide a diagnostic tool for church planters to evaluate potential team members in light of the eight Barnabas Factors.

Why Did I Write This Book?

I have taught church planting and evangelism courses in evangelical institutions for ten years; I have also served with several church planting teams and with the largest Protestant evangelical mission agency in North America. These experiences made me aware of the lack of

---

[7] Because I believe that all church planters are missionaries in the biblical sense, throughout this work I will use the terms church planter and missionary interchangeably.

quality church planting resources addressing church planting teams. This work is written to meet this need in global church planting circles today—to challenge and encourage readers in the area of developing biblically-based teams.

This dearth of information addressing church planting teams was a major factor driving the writing of this book. I have likened this particular aspect of church planting to a desert. Church planters wander in need of something to quench their thirst, yet very few resources exist to assist them in this area of their journey. Desperate times call for desperate measures.

In light of this crisis, I wrote this book with an element of haste. Therefore, I confess from the beginning that this work lacks the illustrative "thrill of victory and the agony of defeat" stories I would personally like to see included. It is my hope and prayer that this work would serve as a catalyst to move other authors to write more and better books on the topic of church planting teams. Others need to share the stories of what is working and what is not working with teams.

For years I have heard of the need to "get back to the biblical way" and send out teams. I have found myself involved in many dialogues addressing the logistical, practical, and biblical reasons for why missionary bands are needed today. I know I have been talking about teams—and I do not think I am alone.

I agree with Elmer Towns and Douglas Porter when they write, "Churches planted by an effective ministry team tend to be stronger, and their future tends to be more secure."[8] It is my desire to see more churches, denominations, and parachurch organizations return to the biblical model of deploying church planting teams rather than solo missionaries.

Remember the Fox—A Parable

Once upon a time, in a forest outside of a lonely hamlet, there lived a fox that had a reputation for sneaking into henhouses at night and devouring chickens. This behavior continued for years until one day, word spread among the chickens that the fox had reformed his ways.

However, there was no truth to this rumor; the fox had actually concocted a sly scheme to attack more chickens.

After news of the fox's supposed transformation had spread throughout the hamlet, the cunning creature decided to venture to a nearby farm for a late supper one night. He took a bath, changed his clothes, and combed his

---

[8] Elmer Towns and Douglas Porter, *Churches that Multiply: A Bible Study on Church Planting* (Kansas City, MO: Beacon Hill Press of Kansas City, 2003), 146.

hair in order to give the impression that he was truly a reformed fox.

"Good evening, chickens!" the fox greeted them in a loud voice. "Come out and visit me for a while as I tell you all the latest news."

Silence. No response from the roost.

"I said, come out and let's spend some time catching up. I have now changed my ways," he wheedled.

Finally, after several attempts by the fox to lure the chickens out by appealing to their curiosity surrounding his new life, one of the older and wiser hens responded.

"Mr. Fox," she said with a firm voice, "you may have changed your appearance and attitude, but we are not convinced that your old ways have departed. For we know your history and are not convinced by a little water and grooming!"

What is the moral of this story? Past behaviors are good predictors of future behaviors. Though the hand of the Lord works to sanctify and mature believers in the faith and bring about life-change, *as a general guideline*, the present and future performance of a team of church planters will be highly influenced by their past actions.[9]

It is a great temptation for church planters to allow virtually anyone on their team. Out of desperation to have a

---

[9] Another exception to this norm is when working with inexperienced individuals. Without previous experience in certain areas (e.g., church planting), people have little past performances from which to draw.

team, leaders unfortunately apply only the "air-love" test as the standard for membership: if potential candidates are breathing *air* and *love* Jesus, then they are right for the team.

When it comes to team development, personal histories are important. The qualities that are desired in a team should be observable in the lives of the individual team members long before the team arrives on the field. Why? Because these qualities and practices will ultimately be passed on to the new disciples and churches.

Before teams are sent, before teams are trained, and before teams are formed, the personal qualities and characteristic practices of the candidates need to be understood and compared to biblical standards. The Barnabas Factors—eight practices found in the life of Barnabas—should be considered as essential characteristics for healthy church planting team members. A potential candidate may have all the desired knowledge and skills for the team, but the lack of one or more of the Barnabas Factors in his life should give the leader cause to pause before extending an invitation to join the missionary band.

What are the Barnabas Factors?

An examination of the life of Barnabas from the New Testament reveals a man who was considered a servant, a teacher, a leader, and an apostle (Acts 14:14). He was described as beloved, a son of encouragement, a good man, and full of faith and the Holy Spirit. He made great sacrifices for the church in Jerusalem and for the spread of the gospel. He was a blessing to others but was not immune to conflict and the sin of hypocrisy.

In this book, the Barnabas Factors are described as eight healthy practices—the outward manifestations of inward character—found in the life of Barnabas that greatly assisted with Kingdom expansion. The eight factors are:

- Walks with the Lord
- Maintains an Outstanding Character
- Serves the Local Church
- Remains Faithful to the Call
- Shares the Gospel Regularly
- Raises Up Leaders
- Encourages with Speech and Actions
- Responds Appropriately to Conflict

The Direction of this Book

The eight chapters each address one of the factors listed above. I provide a biblical exposition of the corresponding passages addressing the life and ministry of Barnabas. Each chapter concludes with a "Points to Ponder for Team Development" section, including questions for leaders to consider when developing church planting teams and questions for teams to consider for continued development. In this section the reader is guided in making specific application of the factor to life and ministry. Each chapter also includes a "Factor from the Field" section. Here contemporary church planters comment on the significance of seeing the particular Barnabas Factor manifested in the lives of their team members. These comments are based on my actual interviews with contemporary church planters. The conclusion of this work provides the reader with a tool for selecting potential church planting team members. This subjective resource is designed to assist church planters in evaluating individuals in light of the eight Barnabas Factors.

What is an Effective Church Planting Team?

According to Walter C. Wright, "A team is a small group of people working together on a common objective, dependent upon one another's contribution, knowing each other's strengths and weaknesses, caring about each other's growth and development, and holding one another mutually accountable."[10] There are several elements of his excellent definition that are beneficial to church planters.

A team is not large in number. An effective church planting team requires intimacy among the members. Smallness is a necessity. Six to eight people would be considered a maximum range.

---

[10] Walter C. Wright, *Don't Step on the Rope!: Reflections on Leadership, Relationships, and Teamwork* (UK and Waynesboro, GA: Paternoster, 2005), 25–26.

The ultimate common objective for a church planting team is to glorify God by remaining faithful to His calling on the member's lives. More specifically, effective church planting teams work to evangelize and gather the resulting new believers into local expressions of the Body of Christ. Biblical church planting is evangelism that results in new churches. Effective church planting teams work to see societal transformation occur throughout a people group or population segment. It is through the preaching of the gospel and the planting of churches that change occurs in the political, legal, and educational systems; families are healed, justice is upheld, and people are set free.

Effective church planting teams consist of members who rely on one another. The diversity of divinely granted gifts, passions, strengths, and limitations means that each member is of worth and of great value to Kingdom work. Each member of the team must also be concerned with the welfare of the other members. Good, open, and honest communication is a must. When one member of the team suffers, the entire team suffers. The team members not only work for the multiplication of churches but also for the mutual edification of one another.

Effective church planting team members are intimately involved in one another's lives. This level of interaction does not mean that members lose their individual identities or privacy, but rather that each member must hold the other members accountable for their actions. A high level of accountability is especially important among members whenever the team is working in urban environments or remote regions apart from close connections with other believers. What team members do in their private lives affects the entire team.

Conclusion

Nutritionists work diligently to assist individuals in making good dietary decisions. They can make suggestions and even develop a regimen of food products that would be the most beneficial for the client. They do all of this with the desire of assisting the individual toward better health and a longer, more productive life.

Even if the client follows the directions exactly as prescribed, the desired result is not guaranteed. An illness can develop. Trauma can occur to the body. Death may come. The future is not known. Regardless, good health decisions should be made now, for they establish an environment that is typically conducive to good health and life later.

As already mentioned, the Barnabas Factors are not eight simple keys to success. Rather, the application of these practices creates a church planting team environment that is conducive to God-honoring missionary work. These factors assist in establishing parameters for the characteristics of effective church planters.

May you and your team be encouraged, equipped, and challenged in this study of the life of Barnabas, a great team player.

Chapter 1

Barnabas Factor #1: Walks with the Lord

"He has told you, O man, what is good; And what does the LORD require of you? But to do justice, to love kindness, And to walk humbly with your God" (Micah 6:8).

"Jesus answered, 'The foremost is, "Hear, O Israel! The Lord our God is one Lord; and you shall love the Lord your God with all your heart, and with all your soul, and with all your mind, and with all your strength"'" (Mark 12:29–30).

During my college years, I taught guitar lessons at a music store in my hometown. Though I always had pupils who wanted to become Eddie Van Halen overnight, I never witnessed such an immediate transformation. Like most music teachers, I expected my students to work on many fundamentals at the beginning of their musical journeys.

I remember one student who, although he was only four-and-a-half feet tall, thought he was the country music star Dwight Yoakam (of course, by the time you added his Yoakam-imitation cowboy hat and complementary boots he was much taller). This student's one desire was to learn how to play the songs of his hero. I began by informing this budding country musician that he would soon learn how to rock with the best of them and would be yodeling like Yoakam in no time, *but* he would first have to learn the basics.

Each week he would be unprepared for his lesson. He did not have much of a desire to learn what an E chord was or how to strum. Though his goals were lofty, he was not willing to stick to the foundational work necessary to achieve his dreams. His time under my tutelage was short-lived.

I greatly fear that for some church planters this first Barnabas Factor—*walks with the Lord*—is one that will be glossed over quickly and given little attention. The passion to plant churches and accomplish lofty goals for the Lord will overshadow the need to focus on the fundamentals. *This factor is the foundation upon which the rest of the Barnabas Factors stand.*

Accomplishing great things for the Lord is never to interfere with the team's walk with the Lord. Our Father does not need one specific team to accomplish His plans; He can use others if necessary. Saul was the first king of Israel but was eventually rejected by God. His actions indicate that he believed accomplishing great things for the Lord was better than obedience to His commands. Following one such act, the prophet Samuel approached Saul with the news of God's rejection when he stated: "Has the Lord as much delight in burnt offerings and sacrifices as in obeying the voice of the Lord? Behold, to obey is better than sacrifice, and to heed than the fat of rams" (1 Sam.15:22).

Effective church planting team members understand that God desires their upright walk with Him more than He desires their accomplishments for the Kingdom. By understanding this fact, the team must place a high priority on each member "walking in the light" as He is in the light. For it is out of this individual intimate fellowship that the members are able to have the necessary healthy fellowship with one another (1 John 1:7) and to function as an effective church planting team.

Since having an upright walk with the Lord is vital to the Christian life, church planters should never view themselves as exceptions to this standard. Of all people, missionaries should be walking in close fellowship with the Father. It is during the church planting days that they will find themselves on the front lines of significant spiritual warfare. They will find themselves addressing issues relating to team conflict. And many times they will find themselves questioning whether or not they should even continue in the ministry. Walking uprightly with the Lord enables the team members to know how to live in relation *to God, to other team members,* and *to those outside the Kingdom of God.*

In Relation to God

A simple reading of the book of Acts reveals that Barnabas had a significant walk with God. It was out of this relationship that he was able to maintain his outstanding character and service to the local church. It was out of this walk with God that he remained faithful to the calling on his life, spoke the truth in love, was involved in sharing the gospel, saw the value of raising up leaders, was an encourager, and responded appropriately to conflict. Luke also records three other significant insights concerning an intimate walk with the Lord: It is *a requirement for all leaders, a means by which the Holy Spirit accomplishes the miraculous,* and *a way to discern the work of the Lord.*

A requirement for all leaders. Having a significant walk with the Lord was required of all the leaders in the churches. It was out of this intimate fellowship that the Spirit spoke to the believers in Antioch commanding them: "Set apart for Me Barnabas and Saul for the work to which I have called them" (Acts 13:2). It is highly doubtful that Barnabas would have been selected to go on this missionary journey if he had not had a significant walk with the Lord.

A means by which the Spirit accomplishes the miraculous. Walking uprightly with the Lord enabled God to work through Barnabas to accomplish great miracles. At the Jerusalem Council (Acts 15), Paul and Barnabas were called to give an account of the working of the Holy Spirit among the Gentiles. Luke notes that the whole assembly became silent and listened to them describing the signs and wonders that God accomplished through them among the Gentiles (Acts 15:12). If Barnabas had grieved the Spirit or quenched the Spirit in his life or if he had not maintained an upright walk with God, the Lord would not have worked through him in such a magnificent way to bring the Gentiles to faith in Christ.

A way to discern the work of the Lord. The third significant value for church planting team members maintaining an upright walk with the Lord is that the resulting life enables the team to see God's hand at work and to know how to respond appropriately. When Barnabas arrived in Antioch and began observing the new believers, it is recorded that he saw the grace of God and was excited. Luke notes that Barnabas encouraged all of them to remain true to the Lord with a resolute heart (Acts 11:23). Following this observation and encouragement, "considerable numbers were brought to the Lord" (Acts 11:24). Barnabas was able to see God's hand working in this newly planted church, and he knew how to respond appropriately to see the word of God continue to spread among them.

In Relation to Other Team Members

When team members seek to love God with all of their heart, soul, mind, and strength (Mark 12:30), it affects their relationships with one another in a dynamic and positive manner. The ability to maintain social harmony and servant leadership only comes from a supernaturally empowered team. Apart from the Holy Spirit filling each member, a team can do nothing significant for the advancement of the Kingdom. Jesus told His followers to remain in Him, for apart from Him nothing can be accomplished (John 15:4–5). Following this great exhortation, Jesus immediately commanded His followers to "love one another" (John

15:12). The connection between these two commands should not be overlooked. For it is only as the team members daily die to self and take up the cross that they are able to relate appropriately to one another. An intimate walk with the Lord also appears to have the following benefits in relation to other team members: *It makes one lovable, it makes one trustworthy and reliable*, and *it provides an attitude of encouragement.*

It makes one lovable. Having an upright walk with God makes a person lovable. It was said that Barnabas and Paul were "beloved" (Acts 15:25). If something in Barnabas's life kept him from having a good relationship with the brothers and sisters, Luke never would have described him as one who was beloved. A great love flowed in the hearts of the brothers and sisters for Barnabas.

It makes one trustworthy and reliable. Having a faithful walk with the Lord makes a person trustworthy and reliable. Sometime after the planting of the church in Antioch, some Jerusalem prophets arrived in Antioch and predicted a severe famine across the Roman world (Acts 11:28). The church decided to respond by sending a financial gift to assist the brothers who lived in Judea (Acts 11:29). Barnabas and Saul were chosen by the church to be the ones to deliver this gift (Acts 11:30). If the people did not see Barnabas as one who was trustworthy and as one who was reliable, they never would have selected him to be the transporter of such a precious treasure. If Barnabas did not have a good relationship with the church, someone else would probably have been selected.

It provides an attitude of encouragement. Maintaining an upright walk with the Lord keeps a person from being too critical and allows him to focus on encouragement and exhortation. When Barnabas arrived to visit the newly planted church in Antioch, he encouraged the believers to remain true to the Lord with a firm resolve of the heart (Acts 11:23). Though it is speculation, there were probably ministries and organizations in the Antioch church that were not as well developed as those found in the Jerusalem church. These new believers probably did not do things with the same degree of quality as the Jerusalem church. Barnabas probably recognized cultural differences immediately. Rather than being too critical and focused upon the minutiae, he saw the work of God and used it as an opportunity to be an encourager and an exhorter. (Another example of this quality can be found by examining Barnabas's relationship with Mark, which will be addressed in another chapter.)

The Factor from the Field. . .

The following are statements from various church planters speaking on the matter of the significance of walking uprightly with the Lord:

What are some practical guidelines a team can implement to keep each other accountable in maintaining a healthy walk with the Lord?

"Model it and encourage one another to spend time with God and in His Word; take times away together for prayer and personal renewal; make it a priority over the busy-ness and the demands of the 'job'; don't allow someone to serve at the expense of their personal relationship with the Lord and when you see their joy is missing – give permission for them to take a break and to renew their passion for Christ; pray for one another regularly; encourage one another with notes, emails, gifts, and time! Let your team know that they are important – not just for what they do, but for who they are."

"A regularly scheduled quiet time is CRUCIAL! To hold each other accountable, we are doing a daily devotional together, although separately. Every day we are reading a devotional on our own, and we communicate with one another periodically to gain further understanding and insight from each other."

"First, develop a series of spiritual, relational, and moral accountability questions and have that document entered into the supervisory or accountability covenant with each team member. Second, schedule regular one-on-one meetings with team members, and practice accountability by asking a few of the agreed upon accountability questions each time you meet. Third, to the team leaders, I would add: get an accountability partner and be accountable to them as your team members are to you."

In Relation to Those Outside the Kingdom of God

Since biblical church planting is evangelism that results in new churches, team members will naturally spend the greatest amount of their time with unbelievers prior to the birth of churches. It is out of their intimate and individual walks with God that the team members are able to minister effectively to those outside the Kingdom. That Spirit-filled walk does three things: *provides wisdom to engage unbelievers, provides boldness for evangelism*, and *provides perseverance.*

Provides wisdom to engage unbelievers. Maintaining an upright walk with the Lord allows the team members to understand how to relate to those who are not in the Kingdom of God. Out of their relationships with the Lord comes a love for their neighbors. Out of their relationships with the Lord comes an understanding of knowing how to connect with and minister to unbelievers.

Disciple making comes from the Lord. In Matthew 28 the disciples are told that Jesus is the one who has all authority in heaven and on earth (Matt. 28:18). At the beginning of the book of Acts, the disciples are reminded that when the Holy Spirit comes upon them, they will be His witnesses throughout the world (Acts 1:8). Apart from an upright walk with the Lord, church planting teams will not be effective in making disciples. Their witness for the Kingdom will be hindered. The scriptures are clear that Barnabas was full of the Holy Spirit and faith. Following this brief description, the verse continues, "... and considerable numbers were brought to the Lord" (Acts 11:24).

Provides boldness for evangelism. An upright walk with the Lord provides the team with boldness to witness to those outside of the Kingdom of God. In spite of opposition and persecution, Barnabas was able to stand firm in the faith and remain bold in his witness. In Pisidian Antioch, many Jews of the city were filled with jealousy and began to contradict Paul and blaspheme (Acts 13:45). Luke records: "Paul and Barnabas spoke out boldly and said, 'It was necessary that the word of God be spoken to you first; since you repudiate it and judge yourselves unworthy of eternal life, behold, we are turning to the Gentiles'" (Acts 13:46). Even in the face of opposition, an upright walk with the Lord provides the team members with boldness in their ongoing witness.

Provides perseverance. An upright walk with the Lord provides the team with perseverance to face and over-come persecution and discouragement. Soon after the account of Paul and Barnabas turning to the Gentiles in Pisidian Antioch, Luke notes: "But the Jews incited the devout women of prominence and the leading men of the city, and instigated a persecution against Paul and Barnabas and drove them out of their district" (Acts 13:50). In light of this persecution, Paul and Barnabas could have easily become discouraged and decided to quit; however, in the next verse it is recorded that they "went to Iconium"

(Acts 13:51). Despite the opposition, possible embarrassment, and possible heartache, the team persevered.

Conclusion

I have a young willow tree in my back yard. When my wife and I first purchased the tree a few years ago, we were able to transport it home in the back of our car. Now the tree is several feet tall, with the long, droopy branches touching the ground. I remember one particular fall when I decided to prune the tree. The branches were sticking out in various directions, giving it a distinctly unruly appearance.

I had a difficult time cutting some of those young limbs. Several were very thick, and they were also green and flexible. Since my saw was dull, there were times when I attempted to twist and break the limbs away from the trunk. I quickly learned that even though the limbs on this willow tree were only a few years old, they were tough and difficult to break. After a lengthy period of challenging labor, I collected the limbs and stacked them beside my house.

Several weeks later, I returned to those discarded branches and began bundling them together to be picked up by the trash collectors. What I observed, though not surprising, was a great reminder of the biblical teaching regarding the vine and the branches (John 15). The flexible green branches that I had struggled to sever from the trunk of the tree were now brown and brittle. Earlier I could have easily tied some of those limbs in knots without breaking them; now I could snap them into pieces with little effort.

Jesus is the Vine, and we are the branches. When we are connected to Him, we experience vibrancy and vitality. Apart from Him, we become dysfunctional and eventually die.

The upright walk with the Lord is the foundation on which all the other Barnabas Factors rest. Apart from Christ, the work of the church planting team will result in nothing significant for the Kingdom. The team must constantly model before the new believers what it means to maintain an upright walk with the Lord. In light of this matter, the spiritual DNA that is instilled in the new believers by the missionaries must already be present in the team. If each individual on the team does not maintain an upright walk with the Lord, the team is headed for disaster.

Points to Ponder for Team Development

1. How will each member of your team be held accountable for his or her daily devotion time with the Lord?

2. Do you agree or disagree that this factor is foundational to the rest of the Barnabas Factors? Why?

3. What spiritual disciplines must already be in a person's life before you will invite that individual to serve on the team?

Chapter 2

Barnabas Factor #2: Maintains an Outstanding Character

"How blessed is the man who does not walk in the counsel of the wicked, nor stand in the path of sinners, nor sit in the seat of scoffers!" (Psalm 1:1).

"Therefore we have been buried with Him through baptism into death, so that as Christ was raised from the dead through the glory of the Father, so we too might walk in newness of life" (Romans 6:4).

In his book *Moral Earthquakes,* O. S. Hawkins shared the following story detailing an account between Princess Elizabeth and a Soviet leader:

> In 1956 Princess Elizabeth, the widow of beloved King Albert of Belgium, visited Soviet-dominated Warsaw. A chief of protocol was assigned by the government to accompany her to church one Sunday. She asked him, "Are you a Christian?" "Believing," replied the bureaucrat, "but not practicing." "Oh, of course," said the Princess, "then you must be a Communist." "Practicing, Your Majesty, but not believing," he responded with a wry smile.[1]

Unfortunately, many people who claim to be in the Kingdom of God are like the man in this account. Though this hypocritical pattern plagues the Church today, there is no excuse for one who claims to follow Christ to deny Him

---

[1] O. S. Hawkins, *Moral Earthquakes and Secret Faults* (Nashville, TN: Broadman and Holman Publishers, 1996), 19.

with his lifestyle. Paul writes, "Therefore as you have received Christ Jesus the Lord, so walk in Him" (Col. 2:6).

Maintaining godly character is another critical component for the members of church planting teams. Such teams need to consist of men and women who walk in the ways of the Lord, especially when no one is watching them. Patrick Morley in his book *The Man in the Mirror* writes, "When we are all alone, with no peer pressure keeping us on the straight and narrow path, that's when our real character is put to the test."[2] Character flaws buried in the hearts of team members today will manifest themselves in the actual ministry later, usually during times of great opposition. Wise team leaders will look for church planters who have a proven history of maintaining outstanding character.

An examination of the biblical text reveals that this factor of outstanding character was readily observable in Barnabas's life. Luke states: "For he was a good man, full of the Holy Spirit and of faith, and considerable numbers were brought to the Lord" (Acts 11:24). This passage of scripture describes three elements in his character that deserve further attention. Barnabas was *a good man, full of the Holy Spirit,* and *faith filled.* In addition to these qualities,

---

[2] Patrick M. Morley, *The Man in the Mirror* (Nashville, TN: Thomas Nelson Publishers, 1992), 250.

he was also *recognized by other believers* and *gave God the glory*.

A Good Man

First, Barnabas was a good person. Since the phrase "a good man" is used infrequently in the New Testament, it is important to pay close attention to its use whenever someone is described in such a manner. Luke is making a significant point regarding Barnabas. Someone who is described as a *good person* must clearly have evidence of that goodness in his life. Paul writes: "For we are His workmanship, created in Christ Jesus for good works, which God prepared beforehand so that we would walk in them" (Eph. 2:10). Barnabas was a man living out these good works based on his character in Christ. When someone examined the life of Barnabas, it was obvious that something was different about him. A good person usually has at least three things in his life: *a gentle spirit, good actions*, and *good speech*.

A gentle spirit. In his letter to the Philippians Paul states: "Let your gentle spirit be known to all men" (Phil. 4:5). A good person is typically characterized as someone who is a gentle person, not someone who is easily angered or puffed up, or one who walks around with a chip on his shoulder.

Good actions and good speech. A good person is also characterized by good actions and speech. Continuing in his Philippian letter, Paul writes: "Finally, brethren, whatever is true, whatever is honorable, whatever is right, whatever is pure, whatever is lovely, whatever is of good repute, if there is any excellence and if anything worthy of praise, dwell on these things. The things you have learned and received and heard and seen in me, practice these things, and the God of peace will be with you" (Phil. 4:8-9).

The apostle is clear regarding the importance of good actions and speech in the life of a believer. He noted many different activities that would characterize a good person and concluded this passage by reminding the Philippian saints that the things they saw and heard from him represented his personal actions and speech. Paul expected them to follow in his steps as he followed Christ (Phil. 3:17). Paul set the example by being part of several successful church planting teams.

Full of the Holy Spirit

The second characteristic of Barnabas's life from Acts 11:24 is that he was a man "full of the Holy Spirit." Barnabas's speech and actions clearly revealed to the Church that he was truly a man filled with the Spirit. In his letter to the Ephesians, Paul commands the believers to "be filled with the Spirit" (Eph. 5:18). Barnabas was an example of an individual who applied this command to his own life, and the churches knew it. Locating team members who are full of the Holy Spirit requires church planters to look for individuals who constantly yield themselves to the Lord and bear the fruit of the Spirit in their lives. *Death to self* and *bearing the fruit* are hallmarks of this filling.

Death to self. The first characteristic of one who is filled with the Spirit is that he dies to self each day. Paul writes to the Galatians: "I have been crucified with Christ; and it is no longer I who live, but Christ lives in me" (Gal. 2:20). It is here the Apostle Paul reveals that the Christian life is a life that has Christ on the throne of one's heart. Gone are the days of self-sufficiency.

In his letter to the Romans, Paul notes that believers are to present themselves as "a living and holy sacrifice" (Rom. 12:1). This phrase is oxymoronic, for a sacrifice is not a living creature but rather one that was killed and burned on an altar. Paul, however, makes the point that these believers, as followers who are alive to Christ, are dead to the world and are set apart for holy lifestyles and holy service to God.

Bearing the fruit. The second characteristic of being full of the Holy Spirit is that godly fruit is evident in a person's life. Barnabas was clearly not just a man of talk, but a man of action as well. The words that he spoke about God were supported by his lifestyle. Paul writes that the fruit of the Spirit is "love, joy, peace, patience, kindness, goodness, faithfulness, gentleness, self-control" (Gal. 5:22–23). Wise is the team leader who develops the church planting team with those members who manifest such characteristics of the Spirit-filled life.

Faith-filled

Luke also describes Barnabas as a faith-filled man (Acts 11:24). Though there are many characteristics that make up the life of one who is faith filled, three in particular are worthy of mention: He *trusts God for provisions, trusts God with plans,* and *trusts God for possibilities.*

Trusts God for provisions. The faith-filled church planter is one who trusts in God for his daily bread (Matt. 6:11) and understands that God will provide for all needs according to His sovereignty (Phil. 4:19). Church planters must trust God to provide sustenance for life and health, as well as for their emotional, spiritual, and social needs. The life and routine of the missionary can seem unstable at times. Limited resources, isolated ministry contexts, and the stress of the ministry all influence the church planting team. Team members must give evidence of the faith-filled life by trusting God to meet their needs.

Trusts God with plans. The faith-filled individual lives according to God's will and timing. It is understood that all plans (e.g., church planting strategies) are made and conducted in accordance with His sovereignty. Effective church planting teams accept James's challenge and live life by this conviction: "If the Lord wills, we will live and also do this or that" (James 4:15). Just as Paul adjusted his plans to the leading of the Holy Spirit and so eventually planted the church in Philippi (Acts 16:6–10), contemporary teams must surrender their plans to God and by faith minister and adjust their strategies accordingly.

Trusts God for possibilities. The faith-filled church planter is someone who clearly believes that *all* things are possible with God and who seeks to walk by faith. This characteristic is extremely important in the lives of the team members. Since church planting is in essence starting with nothing and moving toward something (i.e., a church), the team must trust the Lord to bring about His will.

The team members must trust that God will bring about the harvest in His timing (1 Cor. 3:6–7). They must take courage that "with God all things are possible" (Matt. 19:26), even when they are working with difficult "soil."

> ## The Factor from the Field . . .
>
> The following are statements from some church planters speaking on the matter of maintaining outstanding character:
>
> **Why is outstanding character important to the team and the overall church planting work?**
>
> *"Great leadership is built on trust. Without character, trust can never be achieved. If you aren't a person of integrity, the effort will implode quickly."*
>
> ----------
>
> *"It builds confidence among the team members. It allows the team and the church to have credibility in the community, among the area churches, and within the body of believers in the new church plant. It allows the team to lead; without it, the people will not follow well. It is the well-spring of good decision making."*
>
> **What are some character traits that would cause you to hesitate about inviting someone to join the team?**
>
> *"Self-centeredness in any form (they must demonstrate a servant's heart); negative conflict with others; a contentious relationship with their spouse/kids/family; lack of cooperation when working in a team setting; dishonesty; addictions; having to be the center of attention; power hungry; and a critical attitude."*

Recognized by Other Believers

On numerous occasions, Luke records the fact that the brothers and sisters in the church recognized Barnabas's character. Descriptions such as "a good person, full of the Holy Spirit, and full of faith," were not doled out simply because of a person's intellect, financial well-being, political clout, or popularity. Barnabas was a man who displayed an outstanding character, and the local churches responded appropriately, as evidenced by their words and actions.

For example, when the Jerusalem Council gathered to debate the matter of the necessity of circumcision for salvation, the whole assembly gave special attention to the words of Barnabas and Paul that assisted in convincing the Council that such an outward act was not necessary for salvation (Acts 15:12). Following the decision, the leaders drafted a letter and sent it to the churches throughout the Gentile world to inform them that circumcision was not a requirement for salvation. The apostles and elders of the Jerusalem church selected some men and sent them with Barnabas and Paul to Antioch to deliver this message (Acts 15:22). In the letter, the church leaders made a comment about Barnabas and Paul based upon their observations. This comment revealed that the church indeed recognized the outstanding character of these men. Luke recorded this statement in the Council's letter: "It seemed good to us, having become of one mind, to select men to send to you with our beloved Barnabas and Paul, men who have risked their lives for the name of our Lord Jesus Christ" (Acts 15:25–26). In such a passage, "beloved" was not simply an appellation to embellish a letter. It was not just a term of endearment, but rather a title that was earned by men who had proven themselves to be faithful to the Lord Jesus and His mission.

A second example of the local church recognizing that Barnabas maintained an outstanding character is that they trusted him with their offering. When the great famine was predicted to spread throughout the Roman world, the church at Antioch collected an offering to assist the believers in Jerusalem. Following this collection, the church selected Barnabas and Saul (Paul) to go and hand deliver this monetary gift (Acts 11:27–30).

The church selected these men because their characters were trustworthy. Barnabas or Saul could have easily skipped town with the money or taken a portion of it for themselves; they even could have delivered only a small percentage of it to the Jerusalem saints, telling others they had been robbed along the journey.

A third example of the local church's recognition that Barnabas maintained an outstanding character is related to his deployment to Antioch. When word reached the ears of the Jerusalem church of the conversion of some people from Antioch, the church's reaction was to send Barnabas to investigate the matter (Acts 11:22). The believers at Jerusalem demonstrated their trust in Barnabas by selecting him as their emissary.

In his letter to the Galatians, Paul described his meeting with James, Peter, and John in Jerusalem. He reports that the apostles gave both Barnabas and him the "right hand of fellowship" (Gal. 2:9). This act was a sign of respect, acceptance, and trust. It was an act that was not entered into lightly.

When selecting members for a church planting team, remember that godly character will have manifested itself in peoples' histories. Beware of potential team members who do not have any believers who can vouch for their consistent godly character across the years. If the person has not proven himself in the past by maintaining an outstanding character as verified by the testimony of other fellow believers, then it is hardly likely that he has the character necessary to serve as a missionary on the team.

Gives God the Glory

Another characteristic of godly character in the life of Barnabas is that he was quick to give God the glory and did not attempt to rob God of His fame. When he and Paul arrived in Lystra, they encountered a man who was lame. Following the healing of this man (Acts 14:10), crowds quickly formed around the missionaries; these people believed the apostles to be gods and desired to offer sacrifices to them. The people immediately referred to Barnabas as "Zeus" and Paul as "Hermes" (Acts 14:11–13).

The missionaries could have easily taken advantage of this opportunity and claimed the fame for themselves. Rather than allow themselves to be exalted by the people, Barnabas and Paul tore their robes in the presence of such blasphemy and quickly revealed their common nature and the truth of God. They began to exclaim that the news they were bringing was good news that called for repentance and faith in the living God (Acts 14:14–15).

Barnabas and Paul were miles away from the churches at Jerusalem and Antioch. They could have taken time to rest and enjoy the praise. After all, their missionary activities had not been welcomed by many of the people whom they had already encountered. They had experienced persecution and verbal abuse. They could have easily rested in the fact that here were people who thought they were something great. But instead of taking solace in the moment, these men revealed their true character and gave the glory to the Lord—and the persecution continued (Acts 14:19).

It is critical that teams consist of individuals who are going to give God the credit for the great things accomplished in their church planting endeavors. Individuals who desire to bask in self-exaltation and accolades from others should not be considered for church planting teams. Effective teams consist of people who are *always* going to point to the Way, rather than to themselves.

Conclusion

In a 2006 study conducted by the Barna Group, only two-thirds (66%) of born again Christians said they are "absolutely committed" to the Christian faith.[3] This statistic

---

[3] http://www.barna.org/FlexPage.aspx?Page=Topic&TopicID=19; [Online]; Accessed August 29, 2007.

represents a shameful condition that must not be reflected among church planting teams. Outstanding character that displays absolute commitment to the Lord is a must. Charles H. Spurgeon once wrote: "May we never be priests of God at the altar, and sons of Belial outside the tabernacle door . . . After all, our truest building must be performed with our hands; our characters must be more persuasive than our speech."[4] Effective church planting teams consist of individuals who maintain outstanding characters, both in public and in private. George Barna is correct when he states: "The kingdom of God is never so desperate for leaders that biblical standards should be relaxed to accommodate a person of skills and high potential."[5]

Points to Ponder for Team Development

1. Patrick Morley writes, "When we are all alone, with no peer pressure keeping us on the straight and narrow path, that's when our real character is put to the test."[6] Do you agree or disagree with that statement? Discuss this statement and your response with your team.

2. If you are just starting to put together your team, are you praying and looking for people who maintain an outstanding character, or are you so desperate that you will accept anyone who comes along?

---

[4] Charles H. Spurgeon, *Lectures to My Students* (Grand Rapids, MI: Baker Books, 1995), 13.
[5] George Barna, *The Power of Team Leadership: Finding Strength in Shared Responsibility* (Colorado Springs, CO: Waterbrook Press, 2001), 88.
[6] Morley, 250.

3. George Barna states, "God always cares more about who we are than about what we accomplish."[7] Do you agree or disagree with Barna? Would you and your team be willing to accept a team member who was highly skilled and provided the gifts that the team lacked even if his character was not very good?

4. How can your team members hold each other accountable for maintaining outstanding character?

---

[7] Barna, 88.

Chapter 3

Barnabas Factor #3: Serves the Local Church

"For even the Son of Man did not come to be served, but to serve, and to give His life a ransom for many" (Mark 10:45).

"But now there are many members, but one body" (1 Corinthians 12:20).

There once was a lady in our newly planted church who set an example of godly service. Every week she would pick up a few children and transport them to our Bible study and worship gathering. The parents rarely attended any such gathering but did not have a problem with their children being present. This lady's service to these children and their parents communicated a great love for them. She never received any public recognition. She was never given a service award. Yet, week in and week out, she would reach out to this particular family and serve them with a genuine spirit.

It is necessary to begin this chapter by addressing healthy service. The way one serves on a church planting team reflects a certain attitude toward others, self, and leaders, including God. Service is so important to the Lord that He said that He did not come to be served, but to serve and to give His life a ransom for many (Mark 10:45).

The call to salvation includes the call to be a servant. Though all believers have good days and bad days, service for the King and His Kingdom is part of the daily Christian life. Effective church planting teams desiring to make an impact for the Kingdom must consist of individuals who have servants' hearts. If team members have non-servant attitudes, their quality of service will reflect what is tucked away within their hearts.

Service is like a mirror, reflecting many things about us. Our actions of service can frequently reveal our *feelings toward others*, *feelings toward our leaders*, and *feelings about ourselves*. Though sometimes we can put on a façade and make it appear that our actions are done out of a heart of a servant-leader, over time our true motivations will become evident.

Service Reflects Feelings Toward Others

Service reflects feelings in the life of the one who serves. First, our quality of service reflects what we think about others. If we do not respect others, the chances are very good that our service to them will be poor at best. On the other hand, if we have a strong attraction to others, our service toward them will probably be above and beyond the call of duty.

Service Reflects Feelings Toward Leaders

Second, service reflects how someone feels about his supervisors. Recently I was shopping in a toy store for a bicycle for my older daughter. One of the store employees was very eager to help but did not display very much respect for the company. He tried to give me a much greater discount than I was supposed to receive on the bicycle. He believed that it would not hurt the employer to lose a few dollars on a bicycle. Needless to say, I did not cooperate with his attempts to behave unethically.

Service Reflects Feelings Toward Self

Third, service reflects how someone feels about himself. I recall when I worked in the fast food industry and had certain "bad mornings." I would come to work with very little desire to do the tasks at hand and very little desire to serve others. When I personally had a bad day and was upset with myself, it was reflected in my service toward others.

No Islands on the Team

"No man is an island." So wrote John Donne centuries ago, noting the interconnectedness of people. God created people to exist and function in community with others. Roger N. McNamara and Ken Davis are correct that one of the qualifications for a church planter is that of service in the local church. They write:

> A church planter should be a faithful member of a local, Bible-believing church. He should be actively involved in ministry and accountable to it just as Paul and Barnabas were. It is that local church which will recog-

nize his "call" to be a church planter and will commission him for that particular ministry.[1]

It is easy to read the New Testament and see the giants of the faith—Paul, Timothy, Peter, and John—and assume that they stood alone, separate from the accountability and community with other believers. It is easy to think of our heroes as independent men-of-steel. After years of watching Westerns and science-fiction programs on television, the reader of Acts could be tempted to view Paul and his teammates as "Lone Rangers for Jesus," blazing the missionary trail and "boldly going where no man had gone before." Unfortunately, the rugged individualism found among many settlers in the early days of the United States is sometimes inappropriately attributed to the apostles. Instead of looking for gold, women, land, and liquor, they are seen as free spirits roaming the known world doing the Lord's work.

Of course, such misunderstandings are not supported from the text of the scriptures. Mark Dever correctly comments: "A few passages in the New Testament seem to refer to the church in the abstract, or universally, but the overwhelming majority of references to the church are to a local, living, and loving collection of people who are committed to

---

[1] Roger N. McNamara and Ken Davis, *The YBH (Yes, but How?) Handbook of Church Planting: A Practical Guide to Church Planting* (n.p.: Xulon Press, 2005), 71.

Christ and committed to each other."[2] Instead of solitary ramblers for the Lord, the missionary teams were involved in regular and ongoing fellowship while serving with other believers and churches.

Barnabas was most definitely a man who served the local church. Commenting on the New Testament believers, Elmer Towns and Douglas Porter observe that the role of community was significant to mission:

> These churches were loving bodies where all persons loved one another because they all loved Jesus. Therefore, those churches had strength because all received love as they gave it to others. Those churches were also sacrificing bodies because all members gave their time, talent, and earthly treasures to serve Jesus Christ. If ever there was a group that meant, "All for one and one for all," it was those original New Testament churches.[3]

Global disciple making is hindered without a commitment by believers to serve the local church. Effective church planting teams consist of team members who are servants at heart. No church planting team member should be an island unto himself.

---

[2] Mark Dever, *9 Marks of a Healthy Church* (Wheaton, IL: Crossway Books, 2004), 149.

[3] Elmer Towns and Douglas Porter, *Churches that Multiply: A Bible Study on Church Planting* (Kansas City, MO: Beacon Hill Press of Kansas City, 2003), 21.

Hearts for the Local Church

This commitment to the local church manifests itself among church planters by revealing that they are team players; it also shows that they truly love the Bride of Christ. Commenting on the essentials of a church planter, Marion G. Fray observes:

> Being a church planter and developer will put the missionary in good standing with his Lord . . . If we desire to join with Jesus in what he is doing, then we must place priority on building the church.
>
> Love the church, for in doing so you shall give yourself to what Jesus died for (see Acts 20:28). The church is his beloved Bride, the plan of the ages, and the reason of history. The coronation of history will be the final reception of the bride and her presentation to the Father as heaven's forever family. The local church is the expression of the life of Jesus in a particular place, the praise song of glory to him. Build it, guard it, seek its completion and empowering as your ministry focus.[4]

Throughout the Bible, the act of serving is granted very important status. Particularly in the New Testament, the concept of sacrificial service is found time and time again. Followers of Christ are gifted from the Holy Spirit to serve the Body of Christ. Blessings, talents, skills, and

---

[4] Marion G. Fray, "Strategies for the Development of the Spiritual Life of Missionaries," in John Mark Terry, Ebbie Smith, and Justice Anderson, eds., *Missiology: An Introduction to the Foundations, History, and Strategies of World Missions* (Nashville, TN: Broadman and Holman Publishers, 1998), 591–92.

spiritual gifts from God are not to be used for selfish gain but rather for the edification of the Church.

An examination of the life of Barnabas reveals his involvement in serving the local church. Such service was characterized by *encouragement, participation, sacrifice,* and *submission.*

The Factor from the Field . . .

The following are statements from various church planters speaking on the matter of the significance of having team members who are committed to serving the local church:

Please comment on the importance of your team members being actively involved in their local churches before serving on your team.

"The people that we have were crucial members in their former churches before joining the team. Their local church service taught them how to be leaders."

"This is absolutely necessary! It is non-negotiable!"

How would your work have been hindered if your team members did not have a commitment to service through the local church?

"The first principle all of us needed to grasp is that the church (local church being the a part of the whole) is the body of Christ, and Christ died for those redeemed and identified as the body. A healthy view and a passionate love for the church must precede taking the steps to plant a church."

Service Through Encouragement

Whenever the reader of the scriptures is first introduced to a person, place, teaching, or concept, he should pay close attention to what the author communicates in that passage. This is particularly important when Luke first introduces his readers to Barnabas in the book of Acts. It is here that readers discover Barnabas's name: "Joseph, a Levite of Cyprian birth, who was also called Barnabas by the apostles (which translated means, Son of Encouragement)" (Acts 4:36).

"Joseph" was Barnabas's original name; he was a Levite from Cyprus. In the Old Testament, the Levites were considered temple officials. They were not priests but were subordinate to the priests and were not responsible for the sacrifices. In his commentary, John Polhill notes that the Levites were individuals who policed the temple grounds, kept the gates, and provided music at the sacrifices and for certain ceremonies. Originally, they were not allowed to own land, but it appears that this stipulation was not in practice during Barnabas's day.[5]

Luke notes that the name "Barnabas" was given to Joseph by the apostles and means "Son of Encouragement" or "Son of Consolation." Such an act reveals much about what the church thought of Joseph. A name was not to be

---

[5] John Polhill, *Acts* (Nashville, TN: Broadman Press, 1992), 154.

taken for granted (Prov. 22:1). Names given in adulthood usually came with respect from the ones granting such names. In order to receive such an appellation, Barnabas must have been encouraging the church for a substantial period of time.

Service Through Participation

Following Jesus' ascension (Acts 1), the Holy Spirit came at Pentecost and a multitude of people became believers (Acts 2). Later, Peter and John healed a lame man at the temple, and religious persecution began (Acts 3). Following their arrest, Peter and John gathered with the church and began to pray for boldness to witness in light of such opposition (Acts 4).

At the conclusion of Acts 4, Luke notes the level of fellowship shared among the Jerusalem saints when he records:

> And the congregation of those who believed were of one heart and soul; and not one of them claimed that anything belonging to him was his own; but all things were common property to them. And with great power the apostles were giving testimony to the resurrection of the Lord Jesus, and abundant grace was upon them all. For there was not a needy person among them, for all who were owners of land or houses would sell them and bring the proceeds of the sales, and lay them at the apostles' feet; and they would be distributed to each as any had need. Now Joseph, a Levite of

Cyprian birth, who was also called Barnabas
by the apostles (which translated means Son of
Encouragement), and who owned a tract of
land, sold it and brought the money and laid it
at the apostles' feet (Acts 4:32–37).

This was not an example of some early Christian communism, but rather a community of believers who were so much in fellowship with one another that they were willing to make significant sacrifices to assist each another in times of need. Here was a community deeply in love with Jesus and deeply in love with one another.

It is in this context of the book of Acts that Luke introduces Barnabas by using him as an example of a good church member. Of all the believers in Jerusalem, the "Son of Encouragement" was singled out as the person who modeled healthy participation among the saints. Long before he was sent out to serve as a missionary (Acts 13), Barnabas was setting a healthy example for other believers. His model of service was commended, and it challenged others to serve accordingly.

Service Through Sacrifice

George Barna writes, "Christian leaders must emulate the example of Jesus and pour themselves into building up and edifying the body of believers so that they, too, might devote themselves to selflessly serving others— this is, expressing the distinctives of a genuine, Christian love."[6] Barnabas was an example of such selfless service. He was willing to part with his own possessions to serve the needs of his brothers and sisters.

The significance of his service by sacrificing his land is amplified by his example being juxtaposed with that of Ananias and Sapphira. Immediately following the description of Barnabas's act, Luke records the ungodly example of this couple. Ananias and Sapphira decided to go through similar motions but deliberately lied to God by withholding a portion of the proceeds from the sale; they only acted as if they were serving through sacrifice (Acts 5:1–11).

Service Through Submission

After the martyrdom of Steven (Acts 7), a great persecution broke out against the church (Acts 8). Some of the believers fled Jerusalem and traveled as far as Antioch preaching the gospel. Many people came to faith in that city, and the Antioch church was born (Acts 11:19–21). Just as the Jerusalem church sent Peter and John to investigate the rumors of a great awakening in Samaria (Acts 8:14), the church sent Barnabas to Antioch to verify the reports of an awakening in that city (Acts 11:22).

---

[6] George Barna, *The Power of Team Leadership: Finding Strength in Shared Responsibilities* (Colorado Springs, CO: WaterBrook Press, 2001), 95.

From the text, there is no hint of resistance or hesitation by Barnabas to obey the church's desire for him to travel to Antioch (Acts 11:22–23). It appears that he was quick to respond with eagerness. Though Antioch was miles away, travel was difficult and at times dangerous, and such a task would interfere with his day-to-day routines, Barnabas submitted to the church for such a noble task.

Conclusion

William E. Goff states that one of the elements that assists believers in understanding God's calling to missionary service is that of input from the local church. He writes:

> Paul and Barnabas were confirmed in their missionary call by the church in Antioch (Acts 13:1–4). Many ministers, including missionaries, have had churches confirm their call to ministry because they had watched how they developed a lifestyle of obedience. It is a further confirmation when they support the missionaries in prayer as they go to the mission field. There is also the confirmation that comes through a sending body which affirms that they are gifted for this kind of ministry.[7]

Barnabas was no "lone ranger" for Christ. Rather, he was a man who served the local church. He was involved in the lives of other believers, and they were involved in his

---

[7] William E. Goff, "Missionary Call and Service," in John Mark Terry, Ebbie Smith, and Justice Anderson, eds., *Missiology: An Introduction to the Foundations, History, and Strategies of World Missions* (Nashville, TN: Broadman and Holman Publishers, 1998), 339.

life as well. Because of these intimate connections, local churches trusted him and affirmed the hand of God upon his life.

Church planters should develop their teams with individuals who are committed to sacrificial service through the local church. Potential team members should be checked in view of their attitudes toward servant ministry. Individuals with a history of encouragement, participation, sacrifice, and submission toward the local church should be eagerly sought after. Missionaries reproduce what they know, and they know what they have experienced. If the desire is to see new believers become fruit-bearing disciples who are part of local churches, then church planters must manifest this commitment in their own lives.

Points to Ponder for Team Development

1. Do you believe that there is a significant connection between potential team members in active, local church membership and the health of the future churches they plant?

2. Aside from the characteristics listed in this chapter, are there other characteristics of local church service that you are looking for in potential team members?

3. How is your commitment to the local church (i.e., strong, moderate, weak)? How about your team members' individual commitments?

4. One popular Christian author wrote: "It is not whether you are a member of a local church; it is all about your character." Do you agree or disagree with this author?

Can someone have a godly character and not be part of a local expression of the Body of Christ?

Chapter 4

Barnabas Factor #4: Remains Faithful to the Call

"When the Lord saw that he turned aside to look, God called to him from the midst of the bush and said, 'Moses, Moses!' And he said, 'Here I am' " (Exodus 3:4).

"And He said to them, 'Follow Me, and I will make you fishers of men' " (Matthew 4:19).

"While they were ministering to the Lord and fasting, the Holy Spirit said, 'Set apart for Me Barnabas and Saul for the work to which I have called them.' Then, when they had fasted and prayed and laid their hands on them, they sent them away. So, being sent out by the Holy Spirit, they went down to Seleucia and from there they sailed to Cyprus" (Acts 13:2–4).

Henry Blackaby writes: "The one God calls, He enables by His presence to fulfill completely his call. Any other assignment offered by the world will always be a huge step down!"[1] The calling in the life of a church planter is extremely important. A church planter in Washington state once e-mailed me, "There are times for most church planters when it gets so tough that all they have to hold to is that there is a God, and He has called them to plant this church in this place." Another church planter informed me, "There are times when the only thing that keeps me from bolting out of the trenches is the knowledge that I don't have anywhere else to go in God's will. When the plant struggles and you are broken, you've got to know that God wants you there."

---

[1] Henry T. Blackaby and Henry Brandt, *The Power of the Call* (Nashville, TN: Broadman and Holman Publishers, 1997), 28.

As a church planting team develops, it is crucial that all the members on that team have a sense of God's calling on their life to serve in this particular ministry. When the life of Barnabas is examined, it is evident that there was a clear call on his life to missionary work. This chapter attempts to answer questions such as: *What is a call? Who does the calling? Is calling static or dynamic?* And *what is the relationship of the team's faithfulness to the calling?*

What is a Call?

Herbert Kane states: "No aspect of the Christian mission is more puzzling than the problem of a call."[2] One of the most famous passages in the Bible that addresses the issue of calling is found in Isaiah. The prophet writes: "Then I heard the voice of the Lord saying, 'Whom should I send, and who will go for Us?' Then I said, 'Here I am, send me.' He said, 'Go . . .'" (Isa. 6:8–9). A call is an invitation to serve the Lord that requires faith and obedience. Though there are numerous passages throughout the Bible that address God's call on peoples' lives to salvation, I'm particularly referring to a call to a particular ministry, such as to serve as a missionary.

William E. Goff notes: "God's call is a sovereign call for us to enter into partnership with Him for the extension

---

[2] J. Herbert Kane, *Life and Work on the Mission Field,* (Grand Rapids, MI: Baker Book House, 1980), 1.

of His kingdom."[3] There are four elements to Goff's statement on calling that are important to remember. First, he notes that God's call is *sovereign*. This calling is not something that is born in the heart of a human, but rather it is something that comes from the heart of God. Paul knew this fact when he wrote: "But when God, who had set me apart even from my mother's womb, and called me through His grace, was pleased to reveal His son in me so that I could preach Him among the Gentiles..." (Gal. 1:15–16).

The second element found in Goff's understanding of calling is that it is a *personal* call. Calling can differ from person to person. The experience of one church planter is not necessarily the same as the experience of another. Team leaders should not base their decisions of who should serve on their teams in light of how similar other people's callings are to their own callings. There is a subjective element to God's calling on a person's life to a particular task. An examination of the callings of individuals throughout the scriptures reveals differences among those callings. For example, Luke records that Paul's calling was so personal that the Lord referred to him by name (Acts 9:4), which is not something that always happened with others. In Isaiah,

---

[3] William E. Goff, "Missionary Call and Service," in John Mark Terry, Ebbie Smith, and Justice Anderson, eds., *Missiology: An Introduction to the Foundations, History, and Strategies of World Missions* (Nashville, TN: Broadman and Holman Publishers, 1998), 337.

on the other hand, a general call was extended to the prophet's ears.

The third element found in Goff's explanation of calling is that it is a call into *partnership*. Paul wrote: "For we are God's co-workers; you are God's field, God's building" (1 Cor. 3:9). Here the apostle reminded the Corinthian church that he and his team were partners with God. The call upon their lives to serve the Lord was a call to serve *with* the Lord. God was working in and through them to accomplish His will on earth.

Finally, Goff notes that the call is for the *extension of the Kingdom*. God does not call people to a selfish task or to accomplish selfish gain. His calling on church planters to a team is a call to Kingdom expansion. Paul writes: " . . . through whom we have received grace and apostleship to bring about the obedience of faith among all the Gentiles for his name's sake, among whom you also are the called of Jesus Christ " (Rom. 1:5–6). Here the apostle reminds his readers that the call to serve the Lord as an apostle (one who is sent to evangelize and plant churches) was a call to be a part of such Kingdom expansion.

Who Does the Calling?

In their discussion concerning the missionary call, A. Scott Moreau, Gary R. Corwin, and Gary B. McGee observe: "We do not find any single method used by God to enact His call on an individual. Calling and sending can come through a specific experience such as a dream or vision, but it can also come through a settled conviction that God places on the heart or hearts of the one or ones being sent, or through a local body of believers assigning a task to a person or team."[4] The Bible makes it clear that it is God who calls people to salvation and service, yet the means He uses to extend that call can differ from person to person. Though the means by which Paul and Barnabas were called differed greatly, both calls were completely legitimate.

On the Damascus road, Paul's life was radically changed. From the Lord's conversation with Ananias, the reader quickly understands that Paul was going to be used by God to stand before kings and proclaim His glories (Acts 9). However, when a comparison is made between Paul's calling and that of Barnabas, no details are given regarding the latter's conversion. It is very possible that it was a much less dramatic process. Barnabas is simply introduced as a faithful member of the Jerusalem church (Acts 4).

So how did Barnabas end up in the ministry of planting churches? Following the death of Stephen, a great persecution erupted against the Jerusalem church. Some believers scattered as far as Antioch and began speaking the gospel there. Luke notes: "And the hand of the Lord was with them, and a large number who believed turned to the

---

[4] A. Scott Moreau, Gary R. Corwin, and Gary B. McGee, *Introducing World Missions: A Biblical, Historical, and Practical Survey* (Grand Rapids, MI: Baker Academic, 2004), 169.

Lord" (Acts 11:21). A report of this great awakening reached the ears of the church at Jerusalem and resulted in Barnabas being sent to Antioch to investigate. When he arrived and saw God's grace, he spent time encouraging the people to remain true to the Lord, to stand firm, and to have a strong conviction of the heart. It was during this time that Barnabas observed others coming to faith (Acts 11:22–24). Shortly thereafter, he traveled to Tarsus and located Paul. They returned to Antioch together, and for an entire year they continued to meet with the church and teach the people (Acts 11:25–26).

Some time later in Antioch, the Holy Spirit called Barnabas and Paul to be sent out as a church planting team. Luke notes:

> Now there were at Antioch, in the church that was there, prophets and teachers: Barnabas, and Simeon who was called Niger, and Lucius of Cyrene, and Manaen who had been brought up with Herod the tetrarch, and Saul.While they were ministering to the Lord and fasting, the Holy Spirit said, "Set apart for Me Barnabas and Saul for the work to which I have called them." Then, when they had fasted and prayed and laid their hands on them, they sent them away (Acts 13:1–3).

This initial trip later became known as Paul's first missionary journey.

Is Calling Static or Dynamic?

Though the call to salvation is permanent, a question needs to be raised regarding the call to missionary service. Is such a calling static or dynamic? Moreau, Corwin, and McGee note: "For most of us, God does not lay out the entire life plan in a single call. Rather, He leads step by step along the way. Many missionaries accept their assignments from God one term at a time, whether that term is a few weeks or several years."[5] It appears that Barnabas may have operated under this paradigm. When readers first encounter Barnabas in the New Testament, he is serving faithfully with the well-established church in Jerusalem. Later, he is helping a recently planted church in Antioch. By the middle of the book of Acts, he is being sent out on a pioneer missionary team to evangelize and plant other churches among unreached peoples. Though the call to service for some people may be static (constant), it appears that Barnabas's calling was more dynamic; his roles, assignments, and responsibilities changed over time.

---

[5] Ibid., 170.

The Factor from the Field . . .

The following are statements from various church planters speaking on the matter of calling:

What is the significance of God's call as it is related to serving on a church planting team?

"If the team doesn't feel called by God to this work, then when it gets hard – not if, but WHEN – they'll be prone to question, doubt, and look back after putting their hand to the plow."

"For the church planter, it's the most significant thing. If you're not crystal clear about that, you'll bail out early!"

When speaking to potential team members, what do/did you want to hear them describe when you ask/asked them about their calling to church planting?

"I want people who understand that their entire life is a mission trip. If they are not 'on mission' now, when will they be? So, I tend to seek out people with a great passion for reaching people with the gospel. I have found that, although we all have this burning passion, all of them fulfill this call differently. Some serve in the background so that the foreground things can be accomplished more effectively."

"I want to hear how the call of God has flowed from their intimacy with God. Church planting is about people – so I want to hear a potential team member describe their brokenness for a people. With a clear call, there is often a clear and compelling vision for personal ministry. I want to know if such a vision has a place in the vision God has given me. I do not want to hear of any bitterness over past ministry difficulties and challenges. I do not want to hear of even a hint of pride."

Along With the Calling Comes Faithfulness

When the Lord calls someone, He not only calls that person to a specific task or assignment, but He calls him to an obedient lifestyle. Church planting teams must consist of members who are living a lifestyle that is reflective of the Lord who called them. The call to serve on a church planting team requires faithfulness in at least three areas. First, the member must be *faithful to the Lord*. Second, the member must be *faithful to the church planting team*. Finally, the member must be *faithful to the Great Commission*. In reality, these three areas cannot be separated. For example, a failure to remain faithful to the Great Commission is also a failure to remain faithful to the Lord; however, for the sake of discussion I have separated these three areas.

Faithfulness to the Lord. History is full of stories of individuals who were traitors. Whether they were traitors to their families or to their employers or to their countries, the word "traitor" arouses feelings of disdain in those who hear it. I remember watching a television show in which a school class was putting on a play about the American Revolution. The entire episode dealt with the inner conflict that one of the stars experienced when he discovered he was going to play the role of Benedict Arnold. Traitors are never looked upon in a favorable light.

Though Barnabas was not an infallible individual, his life was characterized by his faithfulness to the Lord. He is described as "a good man, and full of the Holy Spirit and of faith" (Acts 11:24). Seldom is such a description used in the New Testament to describe someone. If there was one characteristic that marked his life and that was clearly evident to the brothers and sisters around him, it was the fact that he was faithful to the Lord. Church planting teams must consist of individuals who have proven themselves to be faithful to the Lord.

Faithfulness to the church planting team. In the scriptures, those who are faithful are held in high es- teem. Paul writes: "The things which you have heard from me in the presence of many witnesses, entrust these to faithful men who will be able to teach others also." (2 Tim. 2:2). Peter refers to God as a "faithful Creator" (1 Pet. 4:19). The psalmist writes: "I will sing of the lovingkindness of the LORD forever; to all generations I will make known Your faithfulness with my mouth" (Ps. 89:1). Just as God's character demonstrates His eternal faithfulness, His children are to be faithful to their brothers and sisters, especially those serving with them on church planting teams.

Barnabas proved himself faithful to the team on the first missionary journey, and Paul was quick to invite him to embark on a second journey. Luke records this invitation when Paul stated: "Let us return and visit the brethren in every city in which we proclaimed the word of the Lord, and see how they are" (Acts 15:36). Although Barnabas did not accompany Paul on this trip because of the disagreement that occurred over John Mark, the point was clear: Paul understood that Barnabas was highly loyal, and he greatly desired for him to serve on the second journey.

Those developing similar teams would be wise to remember Barnabas's example. It is extremely important that teams consist of members who will be faithful to the team, who have a history of being faithful in their commitments and serving with others, and who, like Barnabas, have proven themselves time and time again to be faithful to their brothers and sisters.

Faithfulness to the Great Commission. The challenge of the Great Commission is indeed truly great. The call to make disciples of all nations requires the Church to remain faithful to that great challenge. Barnabas was clearly a man who was faithful to the Great Commission. After he found Paul and brought him to Antioch, they both remained in the city for a whole year with the local church and taught large numbers of the disciples (Acts 11:26). This fact becomes even more impressive when one remembers that Barnabas had been living in Jerusalem for some time. Following his initial investigation of the situation at Antioch, it would have been easy for him to return to the comfort of his home in Jerusalem. Instead, he remained there for a year to help establish this new congregation.

On the first missionary journey, Barnabas's faithfulness to the Great Commission is observed when he continued to go, preach, baptize, and teach in spite of severe opposition. In Pisidian Antioch, Paul and Barnabas encountered much opposition. Luke notes: "But the Jews incited the devout women of prominence and the leading men of the city, and instigated a persecution against Paul and Barnabas, and drove them out of their district" (Acts 13:50). Barnabas could have quickly abandoned the ministry, but he and Paul shook the dust off their feet and proceeded to Iconium, where they would again preach the gospel. Not long after they arrived in Iconium, some of the Jews from the city of Pisidian Antioch came to the city, won over the crowds, and stoned Paul. He was so badly wounded that people dragged him out of the city, thinking he was dead (Acts 14:19). Again, Barnabas could have cowered in fear and returned to Antioch or to Jerusalem—but he didn't. On the very next day, he left with Paul for the next city to preach the gospel (Acts 14:20). Barnabas remained faithful to the Great Commission in spite of severe opposition.

Teams consisting of members who are committed to the Great Commission will remain focused on the task of evangelism that results in new churches. Such church planters will keep this objective in their crosshairs, even during times of opposition.

Conclusion

I have been involved in numerous ministry opportunities over the past seventeen years; some experiences were more delightful than others. Several times throughout the years I have wanted to quit and change directions. I never did because of one thing: God's calling on my life to that particular place and time and people. His calling is the thing that has kept me going. His desire is for my obedience and not my convenience. I have found myself taking joy in knowing that I'm in His will, and that He has a plan for me in His Kingdom. This knowledge encouraged me even when I faced challenging situations. Calling is essential to service in God's Kingdom. This is especially true for church planting teams.

In his work on leadership, Peter Hirsch writes:

> Scratch beneath the surface of any successful leader, from any walk of life or enterprise, and you will find the common thread of commitment in all of them. That's *why* they are leaders. People will follow those who are committed to a future of unlimited possibilities.[6]

Barnabas was that type of team member. He was committed to the Lord, the team, and the Great Commission. His commitment was evident during the good days

---

[6] Peter Hirsch, *Success by Design: Ten Biblical Secrets to Help You Achieve Your God-Given Potential* (Minneapolis, MN: Bethany House, 2002), 126.

as well as in the days of opposition. He knew that the Lord had not only had called him to salvation but also to the missionary task of making disciples through church planting.

Points to Ponder for Team Development

1. During your next team meeting, have the team members share their callings, both to salvation and to missionary service. If you are just beginning to develop a church planting team, make certain that each member can clearly articulate his or her callings.

2. Has your calling to service been static or dynamic? What about the callings of the members of the team?

3. Peter Hirsch notes, "When you are committed to something, you simply agree to play full out—win, lose, or draw . . . Commitment is as simple as giving and keeping your word. Doing your best. Commitment is doing what you said you would do whether you feel like it or not."[7] Do you agree or disagree with Hirsch's thoughts? Explain. What are your team members' opinions of Hirsch's thoughts? Would your responses remain the same if the team was experiencing persecution or discouragement?

---

[7] Ibid., 124.

Chapter 5

Barnabas Factor #5: Shares the Gospel Regularly

"How lovely on the mountains are the feet of him who brings good news, who announces peace and brings good news of happiness, who announces salvation, and says to Zion, 'Your God reigns!' " (Isaiah 52:7).

"Preach the word; be ready in season and out of season" (2 Timothy 4:2).

I have been playing the guitar for almost two decades. Though I do not get to play as often as I like, I love the instrument and still have a great amount to learn. One technique of playing the guitar includes the "bending" of notes. Following the picking of a note, the fretting hand literally bends the string to raise the pitch of the note. This action generally produces a bluesy sound and is frequently done in guitar solos. The irony with this technique is that, when done on most guitars, it leaves the guitar out of tune. In other words, by playing the necessary technique to get the desired sound, the guitarist interferes with the quality of the sound of the instrument.

Though this irony of creating out-of-tune guitars is accepted and expected in the world of music, there is an irony that I have observed in the world of church planting that is *unacceptable*, yet many times accepted and expected: many church planters are planting churches with little to no evangelism being done in the process. The teams are developing great praise bands, delivering well-polished sermons, and producing a smooth order of service, but there is little penetration into the kingdom of darkness with the gospel. Charles Brock notes: "The greatest need today is for the birth of churches through bringing people to Christ and then guiding them into church consciousness."[1] Biblical church planting is evangelism that results in new churches. It is unfortunately ironic when church planting teams begin churches without this critical component.

It is essential that the church planting team be significantly and regularly involved in intentional evangelism. Though there are many ways to plant and grow churches, the biblical paradigm is that churches are planted and grow through conversion growth. The Kingdom of God only expands when people come out of the kingdom of darkness and confess Christ as Lord. An examination of the life of Barnabas reveals that he was an individual who was regularly involved in sharing the gospel.

The Zeal and Effectiveness of His Ministry was an Outflow of His Character

In Chapter 1, I made the argument that Barnabas's effectiveness in seeing people come to faith in large numbers while he served in Antioch was due in part to his walk with the Lord (Acts 11:24). In Chapter 2, we noted that Barnabas was a good man filled with the Holy Spirit and faith (Acts 11:24). Zeal for the Lord and effectiveness in

---

[1] Charles Brock, *Indigenous Church Planting: A Practical Journey* (Neosho, MO: Church Growth International, 1994), 153.

seeing the gospel spread do not come from someone with a shady lifestyle.

Charles Spurgeon once wrote: "Soul-winning is the chief business of the Christian; indeed, it should be the main pursuit of every true believer. We should each say with Simon Peter, 'I go fishing,' and with Paul our aim should be, 'That I might by all means save some' (1 Cor. 9:22)."[2] The evil one knows that if he can hinder missionaries from doing the work of an evangelist (2 Tim. 4:5), then he is able to interfere with their primary task of making disciples. There are numerous good things that he can lead church planters into which distract them from this primary task. Completing administrative tasks, spending the majority of time studying, and constantly refining strategy can all be listed as good things, yet they can be significant distractions.

Church planters must not be content with accomplishing good tasks, even many good tasks. It is easy for a team to lose focus and substitute the good for the best. It is out of the calling and godly lifestyles of the team members that they will maintain the proper concentration on doing the work of evangelists.

But beyond his zeal and effectiveness, what were the elements of Barnabas's approach to evangelism? There are

---

[2] Charles Spurgeon, *The Soul Winner* (New Kensington, PA: Whitaker House, 1995), 9.

at least five characteristics to Barnabas's personal evangelism. He regularly shared the gospel with *intentionality, boldness*, and *tenacity*. He also shared with *a preference for receptive people* and with *a follow-up orientation*.

His Regular Sharing was Done With Intentionality

As Barnabas and Paul traveled across the Roman world preaching the gospel and planting churches, their evangelism was done with *intentionality*. They did not wait for opportunities to come to them, but rather they sought those opportunities to share the good news with others. In Pisidian Antioch, Paul and Barnabas experienced persecution (Acts 13:50); however, they did not allow this persecution to deter them from continuing on and preaching the gospel elsewhere. Following this opposition, Luke notes: "But they shook off the dust of their feet in protest against them and went to Iconium" (Acts 13:51). After arriving in Iconium, a similar situation occurred—they preached the gospel but fled from attempts to mistreat and stone them. (Acts 14:1–6). Despite the frustration, the opposition, and the emotional, mental, and at times physical harm, Barnabas still looked for opportunities to share the gospel. He was intentional in the face of opposition.

His Regular Sharing was Done with Boldness

Closely related to Barnabas's intentionality was the fact that he shared the gospel with *boldness*. Luke records the following about the team's time in Pisidian Antioch: "Then Paul and Barnabas boldly said, 'It was necessary that the word of God be spoken to you first' " (Acts 13:46). Following the Jewish rejection of the gospel, Barnabas and Paul continued to share with boldness. This resulted in Luke recording: "And the word of the Lord was being spread through the whole region" (Acts 13:49).

His Regular Sharing was Done with Tenacity

After Paul and Barnabas experienced opposition in Pisidian Antioch and similar opposition in Iconium, they ended up fleeing to the towns of Lystra and Derbe (Acts 14:6). It was during this time that Luke simply writes, "and there they continued to preach the gospel" (Acts 14:7). Despite the present opposition and the knowledge that opposition would occur in the future, the team was *tenacious* in sharing the good news with others.

The Factor from the Field. . .

The following are statements from various church planters speaking on the matter of sharing the gospel and church planting teams:

What do/did you look for regarding personal evangelism in the lives of individuals whom you are/were considering for your team?

"They had to have a burden for the lost and unchurched. They had to be friendly and have good relational skills."

"Primarily, I looked for people who had a heart to see people know Christ. I wanted to hear that and see their willingness to act on it."

"The essential, non-negotiable quality needed was an unexplainable passion to see people come to Christ. God can do anything with that kind of passion. Other than that, we wanted a willingness to take a risk in starting discussions and conversations that would lead to sharing the hope found in Christ. There are many ways to be trained and equipped, but there is no substitute for desire and passion."

His Regular Sharing was Done with a Preference for Receptive People

Though the gospel was to the Jews first and then to the Gentiles, it is obvious that Barnabas and Paul desired to preach the good news to those who were receptive to that good news. In town after town they would enter into the local synagogue and share the gospel. Sometimes people would believe. Often the Jews would reject the message and would force Barnabas and Paul out of the town.

After the Jews incited the religious women of high standing and some of the leaders of the city of Pisidian

Antioch, "they instigated a persecution against Paul and Barnabas, and drove them out of their district" (Acts 13:50). Instead of returning and trying to engage those people once again, "they shook off the dust of their feet in protest against them and went to Iconium" (Acts. 13:51). By "shaking off the dust of their feet" Paul and Barnabas obeyed the instructions Jesus had originally given to the Twelve and the Seventy.

Prior to sending out His twelve disciples to preach the gospel, heal the sick, raise the dead, and cast out demons (Matt. 10:8), Jesus gave them instructions regarding their travels and lodging. When they entered a town or a village, they were to find someone who was worthy and to remain in that person's home while they were in that town (Matt. 10:11). Jesus said, "Whoever does not receive you, nor heed your words, as you go out of that house or that city, shake the dust off your feet" (Matt. 10:14). Similar instructions were later given to the Seventy when Jesus appointed them to go ahead of him to every town and place (Luke 10:1). In their instructions, He said, " 'But whatever city you enter and they do not receive you, go out into its streets and say, "Even the dust of your city which clings to our feet we wipe off in protest against you; yet be sure of this, that the kingdom of God has come near." ' " (Luke 10:10–11).

Barnabas and Paul did not venture into areas trying to speculate who would receive the message and who would not receive the message. They desired for everyone to hear the gospel. They recognized that heightened levels of receptivity would result in the birth of churches and rapid Kingdom expansion. They also recognized that churches could be planted faster and could grow at a much faster rate among those people who were receptive to the good news.

His Regular Sharing was Done with a Follow-Up Orientation

The actions of Barnabas and Paul, especially as recorded in Acts 13 and 14, reveal their intense concern for the growth of the new believers. The team understood that making disciples was not the same as making converts and then leaving the new believers to stand on their own. They recognized the importance of seeing the new believers becoming fruit-bearing disciples in local congregations. Their goal was not to see how many converts they could make, how many churches they could plant, or how many public professions of faith they could witness through their ministry. Rather, the team understood that making disciples also included teaching them to obey all that Christ commanded (Matt. 28:20). Though Barnabas shared the gospel regularly, his sharing involved an *orientation toward follow-up*. For him, it was not enough to see someone come to faith through his ministry only to be left alone to try to grow.

At the end of the first missionary journey in Acts 14, Luke reveals that Barnabas and Paul were concerned about the welfare of the new believers and churches. Luke writes:

> After they had preached the gospel to that city and had made many disciples, they returned to Lystra, to Iconium, and to Antioch, strengthening the souls of the disciples, encouraging them to continue in the faith, and saying, "Through many tribulations we must enter the kingdom of God." When they had appointed elders for them in every church, having prayed with fasting, they commended them to the Lord in whom they had believed (Acts 14:21–23).

Barnabas and Paul traveled to many places evangelizing the towns and cities and gathering the new believers together into newly planted churches. At some point along their journey, they decided it was time to return to their "home" church in Antioch. Instead of traveling to new cities on the way back to their sending church, they decided it was important to follow up with the newly planted churches. When they returned to meet with the churches, they encouraged the new believers and appointed elders in every church.

Barnabas and Paul understood that healthy church planting teams share the gospel regularly, but they do so with an orientation toward following up with those new believers to make certain that healthy structures are in place for them to grow in their faith as they bring glory to God.

Conclusion

Tom Nebel and Gary Rohrmayer write that when the energy for evangelism in the local church is left to itself, it will "naturally (and in some cases irreversibly) move toward disorder."[3] Though there are many good activities that church planters can venture into in the early days of their work, evangelism is one of the most important. Planting churches without evangelism produces churches with individuals who are already part of the Kingdom of God, leaving the kingdom of darkness untouched. Biblical church planting is not church planting through transfer growth. Since evangelism is typically the first thing to depart from the schedules of believers, a team must intentionally make evangelistic work a high priority.

The Kingdom of God grows through the making of disciples. True missionaries who follow in the footsteps of Jesus and the apostles are not content with the planting of churches through transfer growth. Rather, conversion growth is the first step on the path of fulfilling the Great Commission. Barnabas is a great reminder to teams that zeal and effectiveness for evangelism must grow from

---

[3] Tom Nebel and Gary Rohrmayer, *Church Planting Landmines: Mistakes to Avoid in Years 2 Through 10* (St. Charles, IL: Church Smart Resources, 2005), 53.

healthy character. Regular sharing must be done with intentionality, boldness, tenacity, and a preference for receptive peoples. His follow-up orientation also serves as a reminder that the Great Commission involves making disciples, which includes baptizing and teaching them to obey all that Christ commanded.

Points to Ponder for Team Development

1. Do all of your team members believe that evangelism must include the verbal sharing of the gospel with unbelievers? How does your team define evangelism?

2. Do you agree with this statement: "Biblical church planting is evangelism that results in new churches"? Explain.

3. For your team, what percentage of each week is devoted to evangelism? Is this a sufficient amount of time for this aspect of your church planting work?

4. Do your present methods of evangelism effectively reach unbelievers? Why or why not?

5. Do you believe that one of the most important tasks for church planters is evangelism (especially in the early days of the work)? If so, why? If not, why not? Do you and your team agree on this matter?

Chapter 6

Barnabas Factor #6: Raises Up Leaders

"The things which you have heard from me in the presence of many witnesses, entrust these to faithful men who will be able to teach others also" (2 Timothy 2:2).

"For this reason I left you in Crete, that you would set in order what remains, and appoint elders in every city as I directed you" (Titus 1:5).

"But when Priscilla and Aquila heard him, they took him aside and explained to him the way of God more accurately" (Acts 18:26).

Like many people of my generation, I grew up with the original *Star Wars* trilogy (Episodes IV, V, and VI—not I, II, and III). Names such as Luke Skywalker, Chewbacca, Darth Vader, Death Star, and the *Millennium Falcon* were a part of my vocabulary. My friends and I would spend hours talking about the movies and playing with the action figures.

One major theme of this sci-fi saga centers on the noble Jedi Knights—those warriors who were able to use the Force for good to maintain peace throughout the universe. Becoming a Jedi meant going through a long process of training and apprenticeship. In essence, the Jedi Knights were raised up through a lengthy leadership development process.

Though leadership development is a major part of George Lucas's epic films, it is also an essential element in the life of the Church. Even a quick reading of the Gospels reveals that Jesus closely mentored His twelve disciples for effective service. In fact, several books have been written addressing the leadership development process of Jesus with the Twelve. The Apostle Paul also recognized the importance of leadership development.

I greatly fear that few church planting teams give serious consideration to raising up healthy leaders to oversee churches, despite the biblical examples of this important aspect of multiplying churches. Though there are many demands vying for the attention of church planters, I believe two of the most important tasks related to their ministries are making disciples through evangelism (which was Barnabas Factor #5) and leadership development.

Patrick O'Connor once observed: "Missionaries holding a high view of a church know that it can do God's work, so they help churches raise up their own leaders, relying on the gifts that the Lord gives the flock to do its ministry. Such leaders stimulate churches to win the lost and to reproduce with its God-given power."[1]

Leadership development was significant in Barnabas's ministry. In fact, there were at least three important aspects of his life related to raising up leaders. First, Barnabas was a man who *spent time with other significant*

---

[1] Patrick O'Connor, *Reproducible Pastoral Training: Church Planting Guidelines from the Teachings of George Patterson* (Pasadena, CA: William Carey Library, 2006), 331–32.

leaders. Second, he *saw the potential in others.* Third, he *was willing to take risks guided by wisdom.* Though each of these three components will be addressed in detail later in this chapter, for now it is necessary to note the significance of Barnabas in a New Testament leadership chain.

The New Testament Leadership Chain

The following apocryphal story has been told numerous times and in many variations, but the point is always well made:

> When Jesus ascended to heaven He was met by one of the angels who quickly inquired about His time on the earth. After Jesus responded to several of his questions, the angel eagerly asked, "What did you do following your resurrection?"
>
> "I spent several days with the disciples, gave them the Great Commission, and then returned," Jesus replied.
>
> Desiring to know more of the details of this global task, the angel inquired, "But what is your back-up plan if they fail to carry out the Great Commission?"
>
> Without hesitating, Jesus simply replied, "There is no back-up plan."

It is because of the faithfulness of those initial disciples that I am able to write these words as a follower of Jesus. Through a long chain of leaders raising up leaders, the original DNA that was passed on to them by Jesus has come to us in the twenty-first century.

Barnabas was also a part of a significant leadership succession. He mentored Paul and brought him to Antioch (Acts 11:22–26). Paul was sent out by the Antioch church, and he mentored Timothy. Timothy was left in Ephesus by Paul to train "faithful men" (Acts 13:1–3; 1 Tim. 1:3; 2 Tim. 2:2).[2] Such a leadership chain reveals the importance of raising up leaders for future possible ministry.

The Wisdom in Multiplication

There is much wisdom in raising up leaders. Effective church planting teams consist of individuals who understand the value of multiplication. Not only does this strategy follow the biblical example, but there is much *strength with multiplying leaders, more evangelistic potential*, and it allows for the *fulfillment of Ephesians 4:11–12*: "And He gave some as apostles, and some as prophets, and some as evangelists, and some as pastors and teachers, for the equipping of the saints for the work of service, to the building up of the body of Christ."

Strength with multiplying leaders. Neil Cole notes the tremendous value in multiplying leaders by reflecting on history:

> Strength comes in multiplication. In fact, multiplication is an awesome power. It is the principle of multiplication that releases the

[2] Adapted from http://www.mentorandmultiply.com. Accessed October 11, 2007.

explosion in an atomic bomb. It was the multiplication of disciples which eventually allowed a handful of disciples to become a thriving church that outlived and overcame the most dominant world empire of all history— the Roman Empire.[3]

More evangelistic potential. Whenever leaders are multiplied, the potential for Kingdom expansion increases. D. James Kennedy writes: "[Y]ou will make a far greater impact for eternity by training soul winners than by just winning souls."[4] Because leadership development is difficult work, church planters are likely to see small gains in the short run. Over time, however, the impact of the new leaders will be felt as their numbers and influence increase exponentially.

Fulfills Ephesians 4:11–12. God gave the Church apostles, prophets, evangelists, and pastors/teachers to equip the saints for the work of the ministry (Eph. 4:11–12). Modern day missionaries are functionally equivalent to apostles in that they carry out an apostolic ministry of evangelism that results in new churches. As church planters raise up leaders for Kingdom work, they are fulfilling part of their apostolic responsibilities of equipping the believers for the ministry.

---

[3] Neil Cole, *Cultivating a Life for God* (St. Charles, IL: Church Smart Resources, 1999), 29.

[4] D. James Kennedy, *Evangelism Explosion: Equipping Churches for Friendship, Evangelism, Discipleship, and Healthy Growth,* 4th Ed., (Wheaton, IL: Tyndale House Publishers, 1996), 6.

Focus on the Few

Effectively raising up leaders requires a commitment to concentrate on the few willing followers. Allan Karr, a missionary with the North American Mission Board and professor at Golden Gate Baptist Theological Seminary, shares the following story:

> In my own life, I have recently been asking myself how I can make disciples in such a way that the new leaders that are emerging from the harvest are passionate followers of Jesus, living lives that are missional 24/7. I recently asked my oldest son (17) and my oldest daughter (15) what were the spiritual mileposts of their journey with Christ. Both of them cited the times when people in our church had mentored them one on one. They reflected that the time spent with them by someone who was modeling a life of being a follower of Christ was one of the events that made the most impact in their spiritual development. Upon reflection, that is true in my own experience as well.[5]

Karr goes on to reveal a key component in raising up leaders. He writes:

> I am discovering that we make a greater impact in the kingdom of God by spending more time with fewer people. This principle was lived and modeled by Jesus, [sic] and the disciples who made the greatest impact in the kingdom later in their lives were the ones with

---

[5] Taken from http://www.churchplantingvillage.net/site/apps/nl/content3.asp?c=iiJTK ZPEJpH&b=2466311&ct=2039049. Accessed October 11, 2007.

whom He spent the most time. Even though Jesus didn't mentor Paul, Paul was invested in and he himself invested in others.[6]

Though it may be uncomfortable on the egos of church planters, healthy leadership development generally requires a significant focus on the few. The paradox of leadership development is that *more* is generally accomplished for the Kingdom when church planters begin by pouring their lives into the *few*.

Barnabas Spent Time with Other Significant Leaders

Commenting on an informal poll, John C. Maxwell states that 85% of men and women who desire to become leaders were originally prompted by the influence of another leader.[7] Though it cannot be stated with certainty that Barnabas became such a significant leader because of the influence of those around him, it is clear that he must have spent significant time with the apostles in the Jerusalem church. Luke notes that it was the apostles that gave Joseph the name "Barnabas." As noted in a previous chapter, such names were not given to adults simply because they wanted a new name. They were given because the name had a close connection with the person's lifestyle. Time spent with other significant leaders would have aided

---

[6] Ibid.

[7] John C. Maxwell, *The 21 Irrefutable Laws of Leadership: Follow Them and People Will Follow You* (Nashville, TN: Thomas Nelson Publishers, 1998), 133.

Barnabas in developing into the trusted leader he was by the time he was sent to Antioch (Acts 11:22).

As I reflect upon my life, I remember enjoying many hours with my pastors in their studies, at their homes, and in restaurants. I know the times I spent with them sharing the gospel and visiting people in the hospital were extremely significant in developing my leadership and communication skills. The time Barnabas spent with the apostles in Jerusalem may have played a part in preparing him for making time for Paul and John Mark.

The Factor from the Field . . .

The following are statements from various church planters speaking on the matter of raising up leaders:

What is the significance of each team member being involved in raising up leaders?

"This is such a great concept, and yet we are weak here. Building disciples and leaders takes more time than many of us can give. Programs don't do it very well. It takes one-on-one time, and we have always struggled with this."

"It is very important to equip others for the ministry. We try continually to give jobs away to others and then move on to other areas of need. This is hard to learn, and it is hard to 'let go' of some things when you are afraid it won't be done as well as you think it should."

"It is HUGE! We recognize that our team members would develop leaders differently, depending on their gifts and personalities. Some would develop through teaching and training, and others through leading by example. Bottom line: We knew without a doubt we had to raise up more leaders to reach more people with the gospel."

"My task has gone from that of pioneer church planter to that of visionary, teacher, and mentor. I believe the 'leaders reproducing other leaders' model is the Jesus-model and is significant and vital to any vibrant church in that:

- *It is self-sustaining.*
- *It facilitates healthy organic church growth.*
- *It utilizes leaders in their areas of giftedness.*
- *It produces more solid leaders over time than any other method.*
- *It gives me great joy!"*

"So, we keep preaching the principle: 'Replace yourself! Never do the work alone. Always work in teams.' When we do this, we're training others to do what we do, but it's still hard for our leaders to grasp."

Barnabas Saw the Potential in Others

Barnabas had a keen eye for the potential in others. His sense of discernment was tuned in to the lives of Paul and John Mark. Barnabas saw something in these men when others were not willing to give them a chance to prove themselves. He was a leader who saw the potential in others to become leaders for the Kingdom.

Tom Nebel and Gary Rohrmayer understand that Barnabas's influence in the life of Paul was of such value that, without Barnabas, there would not have been Paul:

> As John Piper describes him, Barnabas was a "leader maker." God used Barnabas's gifts to create a culture within the church in Antioch that gave a chance to a leader who had apparently been sidelined in Tarsus. After he arrived in Antioch, for a full year this new leader, Paul, worked together with Barnabas, teaching large numbers of disciples. Then, one day God spoke to Barnabas and Paul about taking a fresh ministry assignment to influence the known world. There could have been no Apostle Paul without Barnabas, the leader maker.[8]

Barnabas was Willing to Take Risks Guided by Wisdom

One of the true characteristics of great leaders is their ability to take calculated risks. Such risks are not taken in haste, out of desperation, or in foolishness. Rather,

---

[8] Tom Nebel and Gary Rohrmayer, *Church Planting Landmines: Mistakes to Avoid in Years 2 Through 10* (St. Charles, IL: Church Smart Resources, 2005), 40.

for believers, risks are taken with sound judgment based on the wisdom from God.

In the records of Barnabas's life found in the New Testament, he took at least two significant risks with potential leaders. The first test of his leadership was with the recently converted Paul, and the second test was with John Mark. In both situations, it is almost certain that Barnabas's actions were guided by his wisdom that reminded him of the power of the gospel in people's lives, the faithfulness of these men to the work of the ministry, and their giftedness for building up the Church.

Barnabas risked his own safety and that of the church. Soon after his conversion near Damascus, Paul was baptized and began to proclaim Jesus in that city. Though many were amazed that the persecutor had become the preacher, eventually the Jews decided to kill him (Acts 9:23–24). Paul fled for his life, escaping the city by night and traveling to Jerusalem (Acts 9:25–26). When he first arrived in the Holy City, Paul was not warmly welcomed by the saints. Though he attempted to associate with the believers, they were overcome with fear and refused to believe he was a follower of Jesus (Acts 9:26). Paul's wicked past had both tainted his present and scarred his future interaction with the church.

It is in this context that Luke records: "But Barnabas took hold of him and brought him to the apostles and described to them how he had seen the Lord on the road, and that He had talked to him, and how at Damascus he had spoken out boldly in the name of Jesus" (Acts 9:27). Barnabas's words carried so much weight with the apostles (another example of his influence in the church) that Paul was embraced by them to such a degree that Luke immediately notes: "And he was with them moving about freely in Jerusalem" (Acts 9:28).

Barnabas took a calculated risk with Paul. The common opinion was that Paul was evil and should be avoided at all cost. The death of Stephen and Saul's subsequent actions persecuting the church (Acts 8:3) were still fresh in the minds of the people. What if Paul's conversion had been only a ruse to locate the church? What if Paul was only feigning his salvation and he and the Jews were hoping to infiltrate the church by a Jewish version of a Trojan horse? By escorting Paul into the possibly secret locations of the church and her leaders, Barnabas was taking a risk with his own life and the safety of the other believers.

In light of the power of the gospel and his familiarity with what had recently happened in Damascus, Barnabas sensed the Holy Spirit indicating that it was appropriate to befriend Paul. If Barnabas had not seen Paul's leadership potential, he might have avoided taking Paul under his wing, and the history of the Church would have been much different.

He risked his reputation. By taking a chance with Paul, Barnabas also risked his reputation among the believers. If Paul's salvation proved to be a scheme to capture the believers, Barnabas's influence and credibility would have been reduced to nothing. Despite this potential risk of loss, wisdom guided Barnabas to make the correct decision.

He gave second chances. Barnabas was willing to take risks by giving second chances to potential leaders. Fred Smith notes that good leaders must be ready to deal with the failure of others. He writes: "One of the expenses of training is that you commit yourself to people who make mistakes. Mistakes are simply part of the bill, and there's no way to prevent them."[9] John Mark was one individual in Barnabas's life who had made a big mistake.

On the first missionary journey, Paul and Barnabas took John Mark as their helper (Acts 13:5). When the team arrived in Perga in Pamphylia, John Mark decided to return to Jerusalem (Acts 13:13). This departure from the team caused such a disturbance that Paul refused to take him on the second missionary journey (Acts 15:38). Since Barnabas greatly desired to give John Mark another chance, he and Paul parted ways over this "sharp disagreement" (Acts 15:39). Paul and Silas traveled to Syria

---

[9] Fred Smith, "Training the Core Workers," [on-line] http://www.christianitytoday.com/bcl/areas/teamdevelopment/articles/08 2405.html. Accessed 1/3/2007.

and Cilicia while Barnabas and John Mark ventured to Cyprus.

The unfortunate irony in this conflict is that even though Paul was given a chance before the apostles, he was unwilling to extend a second chance to John Mark, despite the advocacy of Barnabas. The one who had successfully defended Paul before the apostles defended John Mark before Paul, yet with no success. Though it cannot be stated with certainty that Barnabas's work in John Mark's life assisted him in becoming a better leader, it is definite that Paul and John Mark later mended their severed ties. At the conclusion of Paul's second letter to Timothy, he requests that Timothy bring John Mark to him "for he is useful to me for service" (2 Tim. 4:11).

No one knows if Paul's desire for John Mark would have been the same if John Mark had not spent time with Barnabas on their missionary travels. I like to believe that just as Barnabas had an influence on Paul, he also had a similar influence on John Mark.

Church planting teams should consist of individual leaders who wisely take calculated risks, trusting in the power of the gospel in the lives of new believers and manifesting a missionary faith in the work of the Holy Spirit among new churches. Effective missionary teams spend most of their time equipping the few as evangelists and pastor/teachers, empowering the few to serve as leaders, and releasing the few to Kingdom service.

An Excursus on Paul's Approach to Leadership Development

According to Maxwell, "It all starts at the top because it takes a leader to raise up another leader . . . It takes one to know one, show one, and grow one. That's the Law of Reproduction."[10] Since Barnabas was the beginning of a leadership chain that involved Paul, I want to digress briefly from Barnabas and examine Paul's approach to raising up leaders. It cannot be stated with certainty that Paul's paradigm was reflective of Barnabas's approach to leadership development, for Paul's approach may have been very different or even evolved over time. Neither can it be stated that Barnabas had no influence on Paul's approach to raising up leaders. It does appear that Paul continued a similar pattern that was modeled by Jesus and used by Barnabas. This pattern had at least three crucial elements: *imitate me as I imitate Christ*; *appoint elders*; and *keep in contact*.

Imitate me as I imitate Christ. It was not unusual for Paul to expect the believers in newly planted churches to live lives worthy of their callings (Eph. 4:1). As a model for them to emulate, Paul offered to the disciples his very life.

---

[10] Maxwell, 141.

This model was applied to new believers as well as to Timothy. Paul wrote:

- "Therefore I exhort you, be imitators of me. For this reason I have sent to you Timothy, who is my beloved and faithful child in the Lord, and he will remind you of my ways which are in Christ, just as I teach everywhere in every church" (1 Cor. 4:16–17).

- "Be imitators of me, just as I also am of Christ. Now I praise you because you remember me in everything, and hold firmly to the traditions, just as I delivered them to you" (1 Cor. 11:1–2).

- "The things you have learned and received and heard and seen in me, practice these things; and the God of peace will be with you" (Phil. 4:9).

- "You also became imitators of us and of the Lord" (1 Thess. 1:6).

- "Having so fond an affection for you, we were well-pleased to impart to you not only the gospel of God but also our own lives, because you had become very dear to us" (1 Thess. 2:8).

- "Retain the standard of sound words which you have heard from me, in the faith and love which are in Christ Jesus" (2 Tim. 1:13).

- "The things which you have heard from me in the presence of many witnesses, entrust these to faithful men, who will be able to teach others also" (2 Tim. 2:2).

Appoint elders. Paul knew that newly planted churches needed to have their own leaders as soon as possible. He was able to find a balance between not "laying hands" on a man in haste and thus sharing the responsibility for the sins of others (1 Tim. 5:22) and quickly appointing elders in newly planted churches (Acts 14:23).

By God's grace Paul was also able to find a balance between not appointing an elder who was a new convert (1 Tim. 3:6) and leaving Titus in Crete to appoint elders (Titus 1:5). It should also be noted that the longest recorded time Paul remained in any given city was the three years he spent in Ephesus (Acts 20:31), and yet the Ephesian church was planted and elders were appointed (Acts 20:17) within that timeframe.

Paul rarely spent lengthy amounts of time in any given city, but he realized the value of raising up leaders for new churches.

Keep in contact. Much of the New Testament is a collection of Paul's writings to newly planted churches. Paul understood the importance of remaining in contact with those new churches and leaders. Whether he was traveling or under house arrest, Paul made great use of the written medium for the sake of edifying the Body of Christ.

When possible, he also returned to visit the churches and the new leaders. At the conclusion of the first missionary journey (Acts 14:21–28), he and Barnabas returned to the churches they had just planted and appointed elders in those churches. Paul's second missionary journey began with his desire to return and visit these new churches (Acts 15:36). Later on, while Paul was returning to Jerusalem, he stopped in Miletus and requested that the elders of the Ephesian church meet him (Acts 20:17). It was during this meeting that he offered them many important words as a part of their ongoing leadership development process.

When Paul was unable to personally write or visit, he was willing to send others to work with the new leaders. Though the New Testament records the names of several individuals who worked with Paul, Timothy and Titus are the most prominent examples of missionaries who worked in Ephesus and Crete, respectively. Timothy was instructed to entrust to faithful men "the things which you have heard from me in the presence of many witnesses," so that these men "will be able to teach others also" (2 Tim. 2:2). Titus was left in Crete to help create order and appoint elders in every city (Titus 1:5).

Much of Paul's work involved raising up leaders. He worked to raise up leaders on his church planting team as well as to raise up leaders in the new churches.

Conclusion

A church planter labored diligently in a community for almost two years. A small group of new believers was gathered together for regular Bible study and worship. Because he believed that the new church members were incapable of taking on ministry responsibilities, the church planter did practically all the ministry. One day, he received a terrible phone call informing him of the need to return home and help care for a dying family member. Realizing his trip would require a two- to three-month absence, he immediately—and belatedly—understood the importance of raising up leaders. Not only had he failed in his ministry as an Ephesians 4:11–12 leader, but he also had planted an unhealthy church. In spite of his desire to see a healthy body of believers, his failure to raise up leaders plagued the congregation.

Sometimes the most important tasks are the most difficult tasks. This situation is definitely true with church planting. Investing in others and working to raise up leaders is extremely difficult, yet vitally important to the church planting task. Effective church planting teams will work to make disciples and raise up leaders from those new believers. The New Testament contains numerous examples of leadership development in action. Life, words, and time were invested in the few that resulted in the multiplication of disciples, leaders, and churches across the world and throughout history. Barnabas was a man who was involved in raising up leaders. His intentional input was especially evident in the lives of Paul and John Mark. The impact of these two men on the Church can be felt because of the influence of Barnabas.

Points to Ponder for Team Development

1. On a scale of 1 (not important) to 5 (very important), how do you feel about raising up leaders? Compare your answer to the answers of the members of your church planting team.

2. What are you presently doing to develop yourself into a better leader? Are you spending time with and learning from other significant leaders, either in person or by phone, e-mail, etc.?

3. When it comes to raising up leaders, are you willing to take significant risks? What are your greatest concerns with taking risks in the process of leadership development?

4. When it comes to raising up leaders, Robert E. Logan and Neil Cole note:

   - People learn best when they see someone effectively *model* the skill or character trait they wish to learn.

   - People learn best when they gain hands-on experience through on-the-job training.

   - People learn best in a mosaic pattern, not a linear pattern.

   - People learn best through *"just-in-time"* training.

   - People learn best when they have effective mentoring relationships.[11]

Of these five observations, which one(s) do you and your team struggle to apply to the church planting work? Are there other observations that you believe belong in such a list related to the way people learn?

---

[11] Robert E. Logan and Neil Cole, *Raising Leaders for the Harvest* (St. Charles, IL: Church Smart Resources, 1992–95), Section 4–6, 7.

Chapter 7

Barnabas Factor #7: Encourages with Speech and Actions

"Let no unwholesome word proceed from your mouth, but only such a word as is good for edification according to the need of the moment, so that it will give grace to those who hear" (Ephesians 4:29).

"For God has not destined us for wrath, but for obtaining salvation through our Lord Jesus Christ, who died for us, so that whether we are awake or asleep, we will live together with Him. Therefore encourage one another and build up one another, just as you also are doing" (1 Thessalonians 5:9–11).

When I was a teenager, I knew a gentleman by the name of Don Downing. "Brother Don" was in his seventies and served as the associate pastor of my church. I sensed the Lord calling me into the ministry when I was seventeen years old; this call was later confirmed by my church family. Shortly after this, Brother Don and I became close friends. He became a great source of encouragement to me, both with his words and actions.

Brother Don and I would speak together often. Without me inquiring into his life, he would willingly volunteer information that greatly assisted me in this calling and new direction in Kingdom service. He would tell me stories about the similar experiences he had with the Lord when he was much younger. We talked about the challenges and excitement of life as a pastor, the value of education, and the need to love people and share the gospel.

Brother Don was the first person to instill in me an appreciation for the value of a Bible concordance. Though I was not expecting it, he gave me a copy of *Cruden's Unabridged Concordance*, which I have to this day. "Next to the Bible," he would constantly remind me, "this is your most valuable and helpful book."

Most church planters can name someone in their lives who at one time was a valuable source of encouragement to them. Of the many things that can be noted about Barnabas's life, it is clear that he was an encourager. In fact, the caliber of his encouragement was so great that it warranted a change in his name from Joseph to Barnabas.

What's In a Name?

Though the significance of his name was addressed in a previous chapter, it is necessary to revisit the discussion related to the name Barnabas. In the Bible, a person received a name with regard to certain characteristics attached to that name. In the Old Testament we see names given to individuals because such names sometimes reflected the nature of those people (1 Sam. 25:25). In the Gospels, Jesus referred to Herod as a "fox" (Luke 13:32), apparently alluding to his craftiness and deceit. Jesus gave Simon the name "Peter," meaning rock (Matt. 16:18); Peter played a foundational role in the establishment of the Church (Eph. 2:20).

Names are usually given to individuals because of the positive impressions of those names. Rarely does someone name a child after a notorious individual. Many times children are given the names of famous movie stars, athletes, or musicians. Consider the number of family names that are passed on because of the fond memories attached to those names. When my wife and I were selecting the names of our three children—Hannah, Rachel, and Joel—we wanted biblical names with godly meanings.

I once heard the story of a great military leader who was responsible for disciplining an unruly solider. When the leader learned that he and the soldier shared the same first name, he quickly commanded his subordinate to "change your ways or change your name!"

Names are important. Though we have come to know Barnabas by this name, Joseph was his birth name. It was sometime after Pentecost when the apostles honored him with the name Barnabas, meaning "son of encouragement" or "son of consolation" (Acts 4:36). Barnabas demonstrated his personal relationship with the Great Encourager by *encouraging others with his speech* and *with his actions*.

It Begins with the Great Encourager

When we examine the scriptures, we come to understand that Barnabas was an encourager because of his relationship with the Great Encourager. As previously noted, he was a man filled with the Holy Spirit (Acts 11:24).

Since the Spirit Himself is referred to as the Great Helper or Comforter (John 16:7), it is no surprise that Barnabas manifested the character trait of encouragement. Our essence shapes our words and actions. Church planting teams need to consist of people who are in intimate fellowship with the Great Encourager. It is out of this relationship that the team members will manifest attitudes of encouragement.

Barnabas was also an encourager because encouragement is in the DNA of the Body of Christ. Membership in the Church requires that all of us be involved in a ministry of encouragement. The writer of Hebrews states: "And let us consider how to stimulate one another to love and good deeds, not forsaking our own assembling together, as is the habit of some, but encouraging one another; and all the more as you see the day drawing near" (Heb. 10:24–25). Barnabas recognized that his relationship to the other brothers and sisters in the church required an ongoing attitude of encouragement.

After the church was planted in Antioch, the apostles in Jerusalem heard of what God had accomplished in that distant city. Barnabas was assigned to travel to Antioch and investigate the reports (Acts 11). Upon arriving in the city and encountering the new believers, Luke's recorded statements reveal the close connections between Barnabas's encouragement, the Holy Spirit, and the growth of the church: "Then when he arrived and witnessed the grace of God, he rejoiced and began to encourage them all with resolute heart to remain true to the Lord; for he was a good man, and full of the Holy Spirit and of faith. And considerable numbers were brought to the Lord" (Acts 11:23–24).

The Factor from the Field . . .

The following are statements from various church planters speaking on the matter of encouragement and church planting teams:

What is the significance of encouragement to the overall health of the team?

"Encouragement is key. In church planting, you have to look for things to be encouraged about and to encourage others about. Encouragement is a cornerstone of church planting."

"My whole personality is built on relationships, and so encouragement is a very strong aspect of our team building. I think that where the main leader is strong is where encouragement will fit into the overall health of the team. In our case encouragement is huge!"

How do/did you regularly encourage the team?

"I always try to communicate how valuable each one of them is to me personally and to the ministry of the church as a whole. I would say this is not my greatest strength… so I need to be very intentional to accomplish this. Involve them in decisions, even if they don't "need" to be involved in them. Help them feel like they are part of your team, not just the team. Let them feel valued by you."

"We give as much as we can as often as we can. I believe in sharing the blessings. We all walk by faith and we have all made significant sacrifices to be on this team. I strive for an "equal playing field" so that everyone feels valued and appreciated. Make sure everyone is taken care of financially and bear those burdens together. Share one another's joys and struggles. Be loyal and never speak negatively about one another to others. Pray for one another. Minister to one another. Serve one another. Love one another and accept one another. Speak the truth to one another in love. Compliment one another publicly. Share the spotlight whenever you can."

"I try to provide positive reinforcement and feedback wherever possible. I brag on the team. I reward exceptional commitment or accomplishment through personal time, a Starbucks gift card, etc. I empower them to lead and succeed in an environment of trust and accountability but free from micromanagement. I pass on positive feedback that I often hear concerning them."

Encouragement With Speech

The writer of Proverbs notes: "Death and life are in the power of the tongue" (Prov. 18:21). Words are extremely powerful. It has been said: "One of the highest of human duties is the duty of encouragement. There is a regulation of the Royal Navy which says: 'No officer shall speak discouragingly to another officer in the discharge of his duties.' "[1] Barnabas encouraged the early believers with his speech. An examination of the scriptures reveals that he spoke words of *trust, vulnerability, consistency,* and *truth.*[2]

Words of trust. After his conversion, Paul arrived in Jerusalem but was initially unaccepted by the disciples (Acts 9:26). Paul (Saul) had been so opposed to the Church that his negative reputation still lingered in the minds of the believers. It was going to take more than just a rumor of his conversion to convince the saints that they could trust him.

At a time when no one trusted Paul, Barnabas was willing to accept him. Luke states: "But Barnabas took hold of him and brought him to the apostles and described to them how he had seen the Lord on the road, and that He had talked to him, and how at Damascus he had spoken out boldly in the name of Jesus" (Acts 9:27).

---

[1] William Barclay in Wayne Cordeiro, *Doing Church as a Team,* revised and expanded edition (Ventura, CA: Regal, 2004), 211.

[2] I am indebted to Gene Getz who listed trust, vulnerability, and consistency in this book: *Encouraging One Another* (Colorado Springs, CO: Chariot Victor, 1981), 55–57.

It was only *after* Barnabas stood up for Paul and spoke words of trust that the apostles embraced him. Barnabas's testimony of Paul's changed life was a turning point in church history. The greatest church planter in the history of the Church—the man who wrote much of the New Testament—had to have someone accept him, embrace him, and speak on his behalf before he was accepted into the fellowship of the Jerusalem church.

Words of vulnerability. Barnabas also encouraged the church by speaking words that revealed his vulnerability. Within the aforementioned passage of scripture, we clearly recognize that Barnabas was putting his reputation on the line when he stood up for Paul. Though he already had spent some time with Paul, he allowed himself to be vulnerable at a time when Paul needed acceptance. Gene Getz emphasizes the vulnerability of Barnabas during this time. He writes:

> Imagine the public and personal pressure on Barnabas; after all he was representing a murderer. A man who had approved of Steven's death and had launched an unmerciful attack against the church in Jerusalem. How easy and emotionally comfortable it would have been to remain silent, but not Barnabas. He went right to the top; asked for an audience with the apostles and stated why he believed in Saul. Barnabas was more concerned for Saul and the Lord's work than for his own feelings and comfortable existence.[3]

---

[3] Getz, 55–56.

Words of truth. Barnabas also encouraged the church by speaking words that revealed truth. Not only do we read of Barnabas standing up for Paul and speaking words of truth, but Barnabas was also a preacher and teacher of God's word. Soon after he encouraged the new church in Antioch, Barnabas departed for Tarsus where he located Paul and returned to Antioch. For the next year, these two men met with the church and "taught large numbers" (Acts 11:26). God's truth came from the lips of these men as they encouraged the local church.

Words of consistency. Barnabas also encouraged the believers by speaking words that revealed consistency and faithfulness. Such consistency is evident when comparing Barnabas's relationships with Paul and John Mark.

Paul and Barnabas took John Mark with them on their first missionary journey (Acts 13:5). Though John Mark began serving the church planting team as their helper, he returned to Jerusalem when the team reached Perga (Acts 13:13). Because of this abrupt departure, Paul and Barnabas would later part company over their different opinions of John Mark's worthiness for the ministry.

Because of this disagreement, Barnabas partnered with John Mark and traveled to Cyprus while Paul and Silas traveled through Syria and Cilicia on a second missionary journey (Acts 15:39–41). Just as Barnabas had vouched for Saul at an earlier time when no one trusted him, now he was willing to speak on behalf of John Mark even when Paul failed to believe in him. Commenting on this matter Getz writes:

> The point is clear, Barnabas believed in people! He believed in Paul when he was rejected by the Christians in Jerusalem. Later he believed in John Mark when he was rejected by Paul. There is no doubt that this quality was a consistent part of Barnabas' life.[4]

Encouragement With Actions

It is not enough to encourage with words alone. Actions must be wed to affirmations. Barnabas clearly did not separate his words from his deeds. His actions were characterized by at least four qualities. They were *substantial*, *sacrificial*, *helpful*, and *exemplary*.

Substantial actions. Barnabas's endeavors were significant to the health and the overall expansion of the Church and the church planting task. Early in the book of Acts, he is described as an example of one of the believers who was willing to part with his own possessions to provide for other brothers and sisters in need (Acts 4:36–37). His missionary activities also required much time and commitment.

Sacrificial actions. Larry Crabb and Dan Allender write, "Encouragement requires involvement in other peoples' lives, a sacrificial giving that refuses to consider

---

[4] Ibid., 57.

the cost of the gift."[5] Barnabas gave up his time and traveled great distances. He placed his life on the line as a church planter. He served with a team that many times experienced opposition and physical abuse. He sacrificed his possessions for the Kingdom and its growth. Barnabas's actions were done with the proper motives. He was not selfish. He was not looking for worldly gain, for he made great sacrifices.

Helpful actions. His actions were helpful because they were done at the proper time among people with the greatest need. Barnabas could have been helping in other areas of the Church's life and ministry; however, he ventured to the frontlines of the growth of the Church. Though he could have remained in Jerusalem, he traveled from there to the church in Antioch in order to help both churches.

Exemplary actions. His actions provided an excellent example for the other disciples. He set an example as a leader within the churches. As a member of a church planting team, he modeled a lifestyle of encouragement before the new churches as well.

Conclusion

The apostles in Jerusalem recognized that Barnabas was such an encourager that they changed his birth name

---

[5] Larry Crabb and Dan Allender, *Encouragement: The Key to Caring* (Grand Rapids, MI: Zondervan Publishing House, 1984), 114.

to a name that meant "Son of Encouragement." Though Barnabas clearly encouraged the early believers with both his words and actions, his source of encouragement did not come from his own strength. By being filled with the Great Encourager, he was able to build up the Body of Christ for the multiplication of disciples, leaders, and churches.

The process of developing effective church planting teams must include an all-out search for missionaries who encourage with both speech and actions. The ministry of church planting involves great discouragement at times. A team of encouragers who speak and act in a manner that reflects the work of the indwelling Holy Spirit is a team that is better prepared for the struggles ahead. Rather than seeing the role of encourager as something to be played by only one team member, wise is the leader who realizes that the ministry of encouragement belongs to all.

Points to Ponder for Team Development

1. Gene Getz developed a scale (see below) that I find very helpful when considering Barnabas Factor #7. Where would you and each of your team members fall on the following scale? [6]

Son or Daughter of   Son or Daughter of
Discouragement   Encouragement
1   2   3   4   5   6   7   8   9   10

---

[6] Getz, 47.

2. Are you looking for team members who are filled with the Holy Spirit, realizing that without the power of the Great Encourager in their lives, they will offer little encouragement to the team and the new churches? What do you look for when looking for team members who encourage with words and actions?

3. How can your team members apply the following principles from Proverbs to their speech?

- "The mouth of the righteous is a fountain of life, but the mouth of the wicked conceals violence" (Prov. 10:11).
- "The tongue of the righteous is as choice silver, the heart of the wicked is worth little. The lips of the righteous feed many, but fools die for lack of understanding" (Prov. 10:20–21).
- "A soothing tongue is a tree of life, but perversion in it crushes the spirit" (Prov. 15:4).
- "He who gives an answer before he hears, it is folly and shame to him" (Prov. 18:13).
- "Death and life are in the power of the tongue, and those who love it will eat its fruit" (Prov. 18:21).

Chapter 8

Barnabas Factor #8: Responds Appropriately to Conflict

"Behold, how good and how pleasant it is for brothers to dwell together in unity!" (Psalm 133:1).

"Be devoted to one another in brotherly love; give preference to one another in honor; . . . If possible, so far as it depends on you, be at peace with all men" (Romans 12:10,18).

"Live in peace with one another" (1 Thessalonians 5:13).

In his work *A Vision of the Possible: Pioneer Church Planting in Teams,* Daniel Sinclair warns, "Probably the biggest source of pain on the field for workers is from fellow teammates."[1] Sinclair goes on to describe a personal situation involving team conflict:

> The first church planting team I led was in Egypt. The first six months as a team were quite rocky, with a lot of dissatisfaction, focused largely on some decisions I made or the way I made them. I sort of expected the problems to just go away, but they didn't. Tension on the team grew worse, and contentiousness became a serious problem. Two or three on the team were making it impossible for me to lead, and it was becoming really unbearable. I still remember the day I told my wife, with tears in my eyes, that I couldn't go on, that I was quitting as team

---

[1] Daniel Sinclair, *A Vision of the Possible: Pioneer Church Planting in Teams* (Waynesboro, GA: Authentic Media, 2005), 31–32.

leader. Three years of preparation at a dead end. I never felt so low. All our hopes and dreams had failed, or so it seemed. By God's grace, we eventually worked things out as a team—and I didn't quit. I grew from the mistakes I had made, some difficult team members changed their attitudes, and soon the Lord pulled us together into a deeply satisfying unity. Before long, we as a team were discipling several believers and a fellowship meeting began. But I would never forget those lows and highs of team life—and I've got the gray hairs to prove it![2]

Conflict among missionaries is a real and present issue that impacts church planting teams serving across the globe. Where there are two or three gathered in His name, there will be friction.

Team conflict is not new to the world of missions. Whether recently in modern day Egypt or two thousand years ago in Asia Minor, teams experience interpersonal tension from time to time. Conflict should not come as a surprise to anyone. Mistakes will happen and misunderstandings will occur. Teams may be composed of forgiven people, but those people are far from perfect.

Though Barnabas is clearly one of the heroes of the faith, we must remember that he was human and had a sin nature. Despite his outstanding contributions to the advancement of the gospel through the planting of churches, he still made mistakes. All teams face problems and chal-

---

[2] Ibid., 32.

lenges to their ministries. It is important to remember that how the team members respond to conflict is critical to both the overall health of the team and to the fulfillment of their mission. While examining the life of Barnabas, I wish to first address the impact of conflict on church planting teams. Then I will conclude with how a team should respond appropriately to such conflict.

Conflict Among Church Planting Teams is Inevitable

Barnabas and Paul were probably the greatest church planting team of all time. Despite the numbers of people who came to faith and the churches planted through their labors, even this team was not immune to conflict. Kenneth O. Gangel notes that "conflict is inevitable where people are interested and involved" in a particular ministry.[3] John Mark joined the duo on the first missionary journey. During the journey, when the team arrived in Perga, John Mark left them and returned to Jerusalem (Acts 13:13).

This departure later resulted in conflict between Paul and Barnabas. Some time after the Jerusalem Council, Paul decided the team should visit the believers in the towns where he and Barnabas had planted churches (Acts 15:36). Though Barnabas desired to take John Mark with them on this journey, Paul did not think it was appropriate (Acts

---

[3] Kenneth O. Gangel, *Team Leadership in Christian Ministry,* revised, (Chicago, IL: Moody, 1997), 188.

15:36–38). Believing John Mark's departure was an act of desertion and hindrance to the ministry, he refused to travel with John Mark. The conflict became so intense that Paul and Barnabas parted ways, with Paul forming a team with Silas and Barnabas partnering with John Mark (Acts 15:39–40).

Not All Conflict is Bad

Though the presence of conflict can result from sin that requires repentance, conflict does not always guarantee the presence of sin. Though Luke does record that "a sharp disagreement" occurred between Paul and Barnabas over John Mark (Acts 15:39), he does not conclude that sin was present. Following the division, Paul and Silas depart, "committed by the brethren to the grace of the Lord" (Acts 15:40).

Sometimes Teams Have to Separate for the Sake of the Kingdom

Gangel writes: "We should be prepared to recognize that positive results can occur when two people who are interested in the ministry have strongly differing viewpoints on an important issue."[4] Though it was probably a difficult decision to part ways, Paul and Barnabas's separation resulted in the word of the Lord continuing to spread. Paul eventually traveled with Silas to Philippi and

---

[4]Ibid., 189.

numerous other cities, planting many churches. Though Luke does not record the details of Barnabas and John Mark's travels, they did venture to Cyprus (Acts 15:39).

During times of conflict, fellowship should not be severed. When Paul wrote to the Corinthians around AD 56–57, Barnabas was still living and laboring as an apostle (1 Cor. 9:5–6). From this reference to Barnabas in the Corinthian correspondence, the conclusion can be made that the division did not sever the friendship between Paul and Barnabas. Also, the connection between Paul and John Mark apparently continued (Col. 4:10). In his second letter to Timothy, Paul writes that John Mark was "useful to me for service" (2 Tim. 4:11).

Even in the Old Testament, separation appears to be encouraged at times for the sake of fellowship. In Genesis 13, the growing families of Abram and Lot were beginning to rub against each other. Both Abram and Lot had a large number of flocks, herds, and tents, so much so that "the land could not sustain them while dwelling together, for their possessions were so great that they were not able to remain together" (Gen. 13:6). Soon quarreling began between the herdsmen of Abram and Lot (Gen. 13:7). It is fascinating to note that also included in this text is the simple statement: "Now the Canaanite and the Perizzite were dwelling then in the land" (Gen. 13:7). Following this description of the residents of the region, Abram approached Lot to inform him that it would be best for them to separate (Gen. 13:8–9).

Though it is not clear from the text, Abram may have recognized that the Canaanites and Perizzites were observing this conflict and tension; he may have believed that this friction would be a poor witness for the Lord. What is clear is that he did not desire to quarrel with Lot (Gen.13:8). He recognized the problems, and the end result was a separation of the two parties.

The Factor from the Field . . .

The following are statements from various church planters
speaking on the matter of responding appropriately to conflict:

**How does your team respond when someone on the team
makes a serious mistake?**

*"Most of our difficulties are relational and require healthy com-
munication and honesty as we share our feelings and concerns,
and then learn to work together and to love one another more fully.
There was one team member early in our ministry that had to
leave for various reasons. It wasn't working out, and the expectations were unhealthy and unrealistic for our church to provide
what she believed she needed."*

----

*"Upfront, we tell people that ministry is a risk. It is a risk and we
may goof up, fail, or not get the results we want. Teach this before
they make mistakes and remind them after it happens as well."*

**What are some practical action steps that church planting
teams need to consider when a team member makes a
serious mistake?**

*"Hold them accountable for their actions and for the necessity to
change. Support them and check on them periodically to see how
things are going. If there is an unrepentant spirit or an unwilling-
ness to address the issue, then they will need to step down from the
team."*

----

*"First, communicate with the person privately, honestly, and
openly to get the full story. Second, state clearly what action must
be taken and why it must be (you should have already set clear
expectations that this person knows they violated). Third, reaffirm
your love for the person and desire to help them. Fourth, keep the
issue private (unless it's a public situation that must be addressed
and then do so with discretion). Fifth, don't gossip about the
situation. Finally, depending on the severity of the mistake,
whenever possible you need to give people who are repentant a
second chance."*

Even the Most Godly Members of Your Team Will Let You Down

Paul also experienced great disappointment with Barnabas in conjunction with Peter's refusal to fellowship with the Gentiles. In Galatians 2, Paul addressed the fact that Peter and he experienced conflict because of Peter's hypocrisy (Gal. 2:11–12). Because Peter was afraid of those with the "party of the circumcision," he separated himself from eating with the Gentiles. Apparently his withdrawal was very influential on the lives of others because Paul wrote, "The rest of the Jews joined him in hypocrisy, with the result that even Barnabas was carried away by their hypocrisy" (Gal. 2:13). Paul's use of the word "even" reveals his own surprise when the Son of Encouragement went astray.

Responding Appropriately to Team Conflict

We know that virtually all church planting teams will experience conflict; what is important, then, is that the team members prepare themselves in advance to deal with conflict in a godly manner. Team members must remember such days will arise and, as they respond to conflict, they should keep in mind the following exhortation: Let everything be done *out of love, for the sake of the Kingdom, as a witness for the Lord, out of a spirit of humility and servanthood*, and *in seeking the best for the other team members*.

Let Everything Be Done Out of Love

A famous boxer is noted for saying, "Let the other guy have what he wants before the fight. Once the bell rings he's gonna be disappointed anyway." Though this statement may reveal a philosophy in the boxing ring, such an attitude must not be allowed to enter into times of conflict with brothers and sisters in Christ. Before conflict gets out of hand and results in sinful acts, team members must remember that the things they say, the actions they take, and the decisions they make are to be done out of love for one another, their love for God, and their love for the unbelievers. Paul writes: "Be devoted to one another in brotherly love; give preference to one another in honor" (Rom. 12:10).

Let Everything Be Done for the Sake of the Kingdom

Team members must remember that God has called them to carry the gospel across the world to make disciples and to plant churches. They are Kingdom citizens who must live in accordance with a Kingdom ethic. Though times of conflict will arise, church planting team members must remember that they are to quickly resolve any conflicts and continue in preaching the good news of the Kingdom. Barnabas and Paul chose to resolve their conflict over John Mark by parting ways, but both teams continued to work in obedience to the Great Commission.

Let Everything Be Done as a Witness for the Lord

Teams must be cautious in the decisions they make when handling conflict because the world is watching them. Words (spoken and unspoken) and acts (accomplished and unaccomplished) communicate much to the world at large. The team members are constantly making an impression on the people around them. How they respond in their days of conflict will be a witness for the Lord they serve.

Let Everything Be Done Out of a Spirit of Humility and Servanthood

Team members should think more highly of the other person than of themselves. If they approach conflict with a servant's heart and with a spirit of humility and prayer, the decisions made in an attempt to resolve the conflict are more likely to be godly decisions. Paul's words to the church at Philippi are very appropriate for teams facing conflict:

> Therefore if there is any encouragement in Christ, if there is any consolation of love, if there is any fellowship of the Spirit, if any affection and compassion, make my joy complete by being of the same mind, maintaining the same love, united in spirit, intent on one purpose. Do nothing from selfishness or empty conceit, but with humility of mind regard one another as more important than yourselves; do not merely look out for your own personal interests, but also for the interests of others. Have this attitude in yourselves which was also in Christ Jesus, who, although He existed in the form of God, did not regard equality with God a thing to be grasped, but emptied

Himself, taking the form of a bond-servant, and being made in the likeness of men (Phil. 2:1–7).

Let Everything Be Done in Seeking the Best for the Other Members

This concept is closely connected to having a proper spirit (Gal. 6:10). If team members understand their ministries in light of the fact that they desire the best for their other brothers or sisters, then the decisions they make are likely to be healthy and wise decisions. Rather than seeking to put their own desires first, they seek to put the best result for the other people above their own inclinations. Sometimes this "best result " means expecting confession and repentance from an erring individual.

Conclusion

Conflict will come to all church planting teams; what matters is how those teams respond in such difficult times. Barnabas was an apostle who was great in advancing the Kingdom but also one who was not immune to conflict. His desire to work with John Mark and his hypocrisy in Antioch caused much tension between Paul and him.

As teams enter into stressful times, the members must constantly remember their witness before others and seek to treat one another with a Christ-like love. Being aware of conflict and addressing it in an appropriate manner can make or break a team and its labors for the Lord.

Points to Ponder for Team Development

1. Do you agree or disagree with the statement: "Conflict is not necessarily sinful"? Explain your response.

2. Is your team presently going through a time of conflict? If so, what specific steps are you working through in order to resolve the conflict? Do you believe you and your teammates are responding appropriately to conflict?

3. Is there unresolved conflict among your team members that has been passed over and supposedly "forgotten"? If so, use this question as an opportunity to return to that matter and address it in an appropriate manner.

4. Kenneth O. Gangel believes that "conflict accelerates as change accelerates."[5] Do you agree or disagree with this statement? If you agree, what are the implications of this statement for church planting teams?

---

[5] Ibid., 188.

Conclusion

"How blessed is the man who finds wisdom and the man who gains understanding. For her profit is better than the profit of silver and her gain better than fine gold. She is more precious than jewels; and nothing you desire compares with her" (Proverbs 3:13–15).

"How much better it is to get wisdom than gold! And to get understanding is to be chosen above silver" (Proverbs 16:16).

May God grant us wisdom when it comes to developing church planting teams! In this day and age of increasing mobility and affluence, local church membership has decreasing significance, and individualism is rampant. Church planters, mission agencies, and denominations unfortunately then turn primarily to resumes, doctrinal statements, and psychological assessments to determine whether someone should serve as a church planter. Ideally, we should hear from local church members and leaders who take the responsibility to vouch for church planters based on what they have observed over time in the lives of the potential team members. Sadly, today we base much of our decisions on the candidates' speaking abilities, musical talents, organizational insights, experiences, and performance in interviews.

There is nothing inherently wrong with evaluating resumes, doctrinal statements, psychological assessments, abilities, interviews, talents, insights, and experiences; I believe they are helpful and necessary for selecting church planting team members. But generally speaking, the North American Church has abdicated the responsibility of being intimately involved in the development of missionary teams. It is my hope this book will be a part of the process of raising the awareness of the fact that *many* of the characteristics necessary for effective church planting teams *can only be truly identified through observing the potential team member in the context of the community of the local church.* Despite the fact that the North American Church in general is not at the point where this assessment process is part and parcel of local church membership, nevertheless it is my hope that this book will serve to assist those developing church planting teams apart from the extended observation time in the context of community. To assist in the team development process, I have included at the end of this chapter (and in Appendix 2) the "Barnabas Factors Standard of Excellence Guide for Team Development" as a tool to assist church planting team leaders.

The Need for Wisdom

Serious fasting and prayer should be given to the gathering and developing of church planting teams. Team leaders should crave wisdom and ask the Lord for it in knowing how to develop the team. This element of the church planting strategy should not be taken lightly. A team can make or break the work. The scriptures praise the value of wisdom and warn of the damage of sin in Ecclesiastes: "Wisdom is better than weapons of war, but one sinner destroys much good" (Eccl. 9:18). The principle applied to church planting teams is simple: Be discerning in your selection of those who will be part of your team. Though they may be individuals mighty in talent, speech, charisma, and leadership skills to assist in the destruction of fortresses in the war for the souls of people (2 Cor. 10:4), use discernment, for their ungodly characters and hidden ways can end up tearing down the team instead. George Barna's words are helpful when selecting team members:

> As you identify people for involvement in leadership teams at your church, you will save yourself and your church much stress and turmoil if you know what you're looking for from the start. You are seeking *leaders*, which means individuals who have been called by God to lead, who have godly character, and who possess the competencies to help people fulfill God's vision for the group. In addition, you are seeking to combine people of compatible leadership aptitudes and who have the ability to work effectively in a team setting.[1]

Recap of the Barnabas Factors

This book has been an introduction to the Barnabas Factors—eight practices that should be found in the lives of

---

[1] George Barna, *The Power of Team Leadership: Finding Strength in Shared Responsibility* (Colorado Springs, CO: Waterbrook Press, 2001), 83–84.

missionaries. There is nothing extraordinary about these characteristic practices; for the most part they are a normative part of the Christian life. I fear, however, that their very simplicity and basic nature may cause some people to discount or even trivialize their importance. It is difficult for a team to take the members of a new church beyond where the team members are in their own spiritual disciplines. People imitate what they know, and they know what they experience by spending time with the team. Effective teams members that desire to model a godly life before new believers must have at least the following practices at the core of their being:

- Barnabas Factor #1: Walks with the Lord
- Barnabas Factor #2: Maintains an Outstanding Character
- Barnabas Factor #3: Serves the Local Church
- Barnabas Factor #4: Remains Faithful to the Call
- Barnabas Factor #5: Shares the Gospel Regularly
- Barnabas Factor #6: Raises Up Leaders
- Barnabas Factor #7: Encourages with Speech and Actions
- Barnabas Factor #8: Responds Appropriately to Conflict

Barnabas Factors Standard of Excellence Guide for Team Development

Though it is difficult, if not impossible, to quantify these eight practices in the lives of individuals, the following guide is provided to assist team leaders in their assessment of potential church planters. The following scales can assist in the overall selection process as well as the ongoing team evaluation process. This standard of excellence guide is also included in Appendix 2 as a reproducible form for ease in use. Though past behavior is not the only or even the best predictor of future behavior (remember, God is in the sanctification business), it is a good guide in team development. The team leader can use this guide to evaluate past and present behaviors.

Please note: The subjective element of this assessment process is intentional. As a team leader, you will set the standards for your team. You know what you desire from your team members. Though your interpretation of what constitutes a high or low ranking may differ from that of other team leaders, it is necessary that the standards for members of your team be consistent for every person. If you have not had the opportunity to observe the potential team member in the context of community, then locate someone who has such knowledge. Provide that individual with your understanding of what would constitute a high or low ranking, and then walk through the assessment process with that individual evaluating your potential team member.

Barnabas Factor #1: Walks with the Lord

- This person can give a clear and concise verbal testimony of a conversion experience.

- This person is lovable.

- This person is trustworthy.

- This person is reliable.

- This person has a good attitude about God, life, and being part of a church planting team.

- This is a wise person.

- This person perseveres during difficult times.

According to the above statements, please rank the potential team member on the following scale according to how you believe he/she manifests Barnabas Factor #1:

Low   Medium   High

1   2   3   4   5   6   7   8   9   10

Barnabas Factor #2: Maintains an Outstanding Character

- This person has a gentle spirit.

- This person has good actions.

- This person has good speech.

- This person is consistently filled with the Holy Spirit.

- The fruit of the Spirit is evident in this person's life.

- This person is faith-filled.

- This person trusts God for provisions.

- This person trusts God with his/her plans.

- This person trusts God with the impossible.

- This person does not rob God of His fame.

According to the above statements, please rank the potential team member on the following scale according to how you believe he/she manifests Barnabas Factor #2:

Low   Medium   High

1   2   3   4   5   6   7   8   9   10

Barnabas Factor #3: Serves the Local Church

- This person reflects a positive attitude toward servant leadership.

- This person is not a "lone ranger" for Jesus, nor an island unto him/herself.

- This person is a member of _____ church (local).

- The leaders and other members of this person's local church speak highly of him/her.

- This person is passionate about the local church.

- This person encourages the local church.

- This person is active in using his/her gifts and talents to serve the local church.

- This person makes sacrifices for his/her local church.

- This person submits to the pastors of his/her local church.

According to the above statements, please rank the potential team member on the following scale according to how you believe he/she manifests Barnabas Factor #3:

Low   Medium   High

1   2   3   4   5   6   7   8   9   10

Barnabas Factor #4: Remains Faithful to the Call

- This person can give evidence of a call to the same (or similar) task as that of the team.

- This person will remain faithful to this call even if he or she does not become part of this team.

- This person is faithful to the Lord.

- This person will be faithful to the team.

- This person is faithful to the Great Commission.

According to the above statements, please rank the potential team member on the following scale according to how you believe he/she manifests Barnabas Factor #4:

Low   Medium   High

1   2   3   4   5   6   7   8   9   10

Barnabas Factor #5: Shares the Gospel Regularly

- This person can share a clear and concise verbal presentation of the gospel.

- This person has a zeal for sharing the gospel.

- This person intentionally and regularly shares the gospel.

- This person continues to look for opportunities to share the gospel even when people are not receptive.

- This person prefers to work among people who are highly receptive to the gospel.

- This person is concerned with making disciples, not simply making converts.

According to the above statements, please rank the potential team member on the following scale according to how you believe he/she manifests Barnabas Factor #5:

Low   Medium   High

1   2   3   4   5   6   7   8   9   10

Barnabas Factor #6: Raises Up Leaders

- The multiplication of disciples, leaders, and churches is a part of this person's philosophy of ministry.

- This person would rather focus on a few potential leaders than spend the majority of his/her time with large numbers of people.

- This person is eager to grow as a leader.

- This person sees the leadership potential in others.

- This person takes wise and calculated risks.

- This person's attitude and lifestyle is a great model for other believers.

According to the above statements, please rank the potential team member on the following scale according to how you believe he/she manifests Barnabas Factor #6:

Low   Medium   High

1   2   3   4   5   6   7   8   9   10

Barnabas Factor #7: Encourages with Speech and Actions

- This person is an encourager with both his/her words and actions.

- This person speaks words of truth.

- This person is not afraid to be vulnerable among other team members.

- This person speaks words that reveal a consistent lifestyle.

- This is a helpful person.

- This is a person who takes on substantial tasks for the Kingdom.

- This person's actions reveal a sacrificial lifestyle for the spread of the gospel.

- This person will set a healthy example for the other team members.

According to the above statements, please rank the potential team member on the following scale according to how you believe he/she manifests Barnabas Factor #7:

Low   Medium   High

1   2   3   4   5   6   7   8   9   10

Barnabas Factor #8: Responds Appropriately to Conflict

- This person understands that all teams experience conflict.

- This person can clearly articulate general biblical principles for how to handle team conflict.

- This person has no major unresolved conflict in his or her life.

- This person responds with love even when wronged.

- This person understands that sometimes teams will have to separate for the sake of the Kingdom.

- This person manifests a genuine sense of humility and servanthood even during times of conflict.

- This person does not hold grudges against others.

- This person truly desires to seek the best for others.

According to the above statements, please rank the potential team member on the following scale according to how you believe he/she manifests Barnabas Factor #8:

Low   Medium   High

1   2   3   4   5   6   7   8   9   10

Overall Ranking

Low: 8-24

Do not select this person for the team.

Medium: 32-56

This person may have some significant struggles at times if placed on the team. Identify the Barnabas Factors where this person scored low and provide guidance to improve. Consider inviting this individual to the team but with strong reservations/conditions.

High: 64-80

Though a high ranking is not a guarantee of effectiveness, it does reveal that this person strongly manifests the Barnabas Factors that are necessary for a healthy team member. Consider inviting this individual to the team.

Appendix 1

Guidelines for Developing A Covenant Of Team Understandings (COTU)

(Taken and adapted from Dick Scoggins, *Building Effective Church Planting Teams,* available from www.dickscoggins.com. Used with permission).

You, in your role as team leader, need to develop a Covenant of Team Understandings (COTU) which will enable potential team members to understand how your team will function. A copy of your COTU should be on file with your sending base (church) since it spells out your relationship with them. Your mentor should have a copy as well. Try to keep this to four or five pages in length. It will generally spell out the relationship of your team members to you, to their sending churches, and to any other agencies that may be involved. You may have a more extensive version for use by the team on the field in which you spell out more details. Likewise those members of your "home team" in your sending church may want more specifics as well. Get help from your church leaders, other team leaders, prospective team members, or your mentor in thinking through those questions you get stuck on.

Consider the following points as you develop your COTU:

1. People follow someone who leads. Share your understanding of team dynamics in such a way that it enhances their confidence in team life.

2. Do as much as you can to enable them to picture what team life would be like. Things like your leadership style, their participation, team reproduction, and how interpersonal relationships will enable growth of all members should be evident to the reader.

3. Keep in mind your audience—the prospective team members. They will likely be looking for two things: (1) security from the leader and (2) freedom to take the initiative. It is not easy to put these two contrasting things together. Keep this in mind as you develop your COTU, trying to balance security with creativity. If you have had leadership experiences in your other settings, draw upon them. Be tactful, realizing that initial resistance often dissolves with deepening relationship.

4. People are drawn to a winner. Use your COTU to share ideas on why you believe this team is going to get into a community (or closed country), stay in, grow, make disciples, and see a reproductive community of believers come into being.

5. If you are in the process of drawing prospective team members onto your team, you should enlist their help in writing the COTU. The more input they have, the more ownership they will have. As part of the COTU, you should develop a one-page team covenant, which defines the relational expectations of the team and how conflicts will be resolved. After your team is formed, those added to the team will sign on to an already-existing covenant.

You may want to get ideas from some other team leaders' COTUs.

You may want to let potential team members know your strengths and weaknesses and how you see them complementing you. Why do you need a team in the first place? People need to be needed.

Specific questions a COTU should address:

1. Summarize briefly (a sentence or two): Where are you going? What is your specific target (people group, socio-economic segment, city, etc.)? Are there any non-negotiables in strategy? (This will be more thoroughly developed in your Strategy Paper).

2. What are some ways that you will be able to get employment for your team members?

3. Who makes life-style decisions? Where to live? Apartment? House? As single families or as a team? What do team members have to agree to before they leave?

4. For those who are supported, how is the support level set? What does this level include? Just personal family needs or does it include ministry expenses? Will there be any funds pooled for team ministry? An emergency fund? Once a church is established, where will their giving be dispersed?

5. How are decisions made?

6. How is conflict to be resolved? What recourse is there if the conflict is with the team leader? (Put yourself in their shoes!)

7. What if they determine that they should not be there after arriving? What is the exit procedure? How soon can they leave? Is there a probation period?

8. If your COTU deals with cross-cultural church planting, will members be expected to learn language?

9. What skills are they expected to have before they get to your team? How do they really know that they are ready to go?

10. What about theological issues? Are there any theological non-negotiables such as charismatic leanings, etc.? What kind of person would be most comfortable on this team?

11. What happens if the team leader feels called to another area and leaves behind a remnant of the team?

12. What provisions are there for sickness, emergencies, vacations, and leaves of absence?

13. Who is the team leader accountable to? How do the sending churches fit into the team's effort? Who is responsible for seeing that the work is kept in high profile in the sending church? What kind of coaching or mentoring are the team members going to get from outside the team?

14. Are there any restrictions on the team for the first year? (Visits home, vacation, training in other places?)

15. How do you envision team life? Will the team meet for worship? Prayer? Training? Socially? How often? Will there be different roles for men and women? Will you accept single women on the team?

16. How will shepherding roles be set up? What if members have problems in their families? Who will they go to? Will there be discipling of younger members by older ones? If a wife is a co-member of the team, who is responsible to shepherd her? In what areas?

17. What sort of reporting procedure will be followed? (to the home church, other agencies, etc.)

Appendix 2

Barnabas Factors Standard of Excellence Guide for Team Development

Directions: The subjective element of this assessment process is intentional. As a team leader, you will set the standards for your team. You know what you desire from your team members. Though your interpretation of what constitutes a high or low ranking may differ from that of other team leaders, it is necessary that the standards for members of your team be consistent for every person. If you have not had the opportunity to observe the potential team member in the context of community, then locate someone who has such knowledge. Provide that individual with your understanding of what would constitute a high or low ranking, and then walk through the assessment process with that individual evaluating your potential team member.

Name: _____

Date: _____

Evaluator's name:_____

Barnabas Factor #1: Walks with the Lord

- This person can give a clear and concise verbal testimony of a conversion experience.

- This person is lovable.

- This person is trustworthy.

- This person is reliable.

- This person has a good attitude about God, life, and being part of a church planting team.

- This is a wise person.

- This person perseveres during difficult times.

According to the above statements, please rank the potential team member on the following scale according to how you believe he/she manifests Barnabas Factor #1:

Low   Medium   High

1   2   3   4   5   6   7   8   9   10

Barnabas Factor #2: Maintains an Outstanding Character

- This person has a gentle spirit.

- This person has good actions.

- This person has good speech.

- This person is consistently filled with the Holy Spirit.

- The fruit of the Spirit is evident in this person's life.

- This person is faith-filled.

- This person trusts God for provisions.

- This person trusts God with his/her plans.

- This person trusts God with the impossible.

- This person does not rob God of His fame.

According to the above statements, please rank the potential team member on the following scale according to how you believe he/she manifests Barnabas Factor #2:

Low   Medium   High

1   2   3   4   5   6   7   8   9   10

Barnabas Factor #3: Serves the Local Church

- This person reflects a positive attitude toward servant leadership.

- This person is not a "lone ranger" for Jesus, nor an island unto him/herself.

- This person is a member of _____ church (local).

- The leaders and other members of this person's local church speak highly of him/her.

- This person is passionate about the local church.

- This person encourages the local church.

- This person is active in using his/her gifts and talents to serve the local church.

- This person makes sacrifices for his/her local church.

- This person submits to the pastors of his/her local church.

According to the above statements, please rank the potential team member on the following scale according to how you believe he/she manifests Barnabas Factor #3:

Low   Medium   High

1   2   3   4   5   6   7   8   9   10

Barnabas Factor #4: Remains Faithful to the Call

- This person can give evidence of a call to the same (or similar) task as that of the team.

- This person will remain faithful to this call even if he or she does not become part of this team.

- This person is faithful to the Lord.

- This person will be faithful to the team.

- This person is faithful to the Great Commission.

According to the above statements, please rank the potential team member on the following scale according to how you believe he/she manifests Barnabas Factor #4:

Low   Medium   High

1   2   3   4   5   6   7   8   9   10

Barnabas Factor #5: Shares the Gospel Regularly

- This person can share a clear and concise verbal presentation of the gospel.

- This person has a zeal for sharing the gospel.

- This person intentionally and regularly shares the gospel.

- This person continues to look for opportunities to share the gospel even when people are not receptive.

- This person prefers to work among people who are highly receptive to the gospel.

- This person is concerned with making disciples, not simply making converts.

According to the above statements, please rank the potential team member on the following scale according to how you believe he/she manifests Barnabas Factor #5:

Low   Medium   High

1   2   3   4   5   6   7   8   9   10

Barnabas Factor #6: Raises Up Leaders

- The multiplication of disciples, leaders, and churches is a part of this person's philosophy of ministry.
- This person would rather focus on a few potential leaders than spend the majority of his or her time with large numbers of people.
- This person is eager to grow as a leader.
- This person sees the leadership potential in others.
- This person takes wise and calculated risks.
- This person's attitude and lifestyle is a great model for other believers.

According to the above statements, please rank the potential team member on the following scale according to how you believe he/she manifests Barnabas Factor #6:

Low   Medium   High

1   2   3   4   5   6   7   8   9   10

Barnabas Factor #7: Encourages with Speech and Actions

- This person is an encourager with both his/her words and actions.

- This person speaks words of truth.

- This person is not afraid to be vulnerable among other team members.

- This person speaks words that reveal a consistent lifestyle.

- This is a helpful person.

- This is a person who takes on substantial tasks for the Kingdom.

- This person's actions reveal a sacrificial lifestyle for the spread of the gospel.

- This is a person who will set a healthy example for the other team members.

According to the above statements, please rank the potential team member on the following scale according to how you believe he/she manifests Barnabas Factor #7:

Low   Medium   High

1   2   3   4   5   6   7   8   9   10

Barnabas Factor #8: Responds Appropriately to Conflict

- This person understands that all teams experience conflict.

- This person can clearly articulate general biblical principles for how to handle team conflict.

- This person has no major unresolved conflict in his or her life.

- Even when wronged, this person responds with love.

- This person understands that sometimes teams will have to separate for the sake of the Kingdom.

- This person manifests a genuine sense of humility and servanthood even during times of conflict.

- This person does not hold grudges against others.

- This person truly desires to seek the best for others.

According to the above statements, please rank the potential team member on the following scale according to how you believe he/she manifests Barnabas Factor #8:

Low   Medium   High

1   2   3   4   5   6   7   8   9   10

Overall Ranking

Low: 8-24

Do not select this person for the team.

Medium: 32-56

This person may have some significant struggles at times if placed on the team. Identify the Barnabas Factors where this person scored low and provide guidance to improve. Consider inviting this individual to the team but with strong reservations/conditions.

High: 64-80

Though a high ranking is not a guarantee of effectiveness, it does reveal that this person strongly manifests the Barnabas Factors that are necessary for a healthy team member. Consider inviting this individual to the team.

For articles, podcasts, book reviews, newsletters, and links to sites related to missions, see J. D. Payne's web site: www.NorthAmericanMissions.org.

This site is devoted to equipping the Body of Christ for the multiplication of disciples, leaders, and churches throughout North America.